How Can You Smell the Roses if the Tops Have Been Cut Off?

By

Margaret A. Gray

This book is a work of fiction. Places, events, and situations in this story are purely fictional. Any resemblance to actual persons, living or dead, is coincidental.

ISBN: 1-4107-4449-3 (e-book)
ISBN: 1-4107-4450-7 (Paperback)

This book is printed on acid free paper.

1stBooks - rev. 6/25/03

Looking around at this state of mass confusion somehow was comforting. My husband was outside moving the last of our things into our new home. He and I had been separated for a few months but decided to give our marriage another try.

As I sat at the kitchen table surveying how and where things would go and fit, I wondered if things would be different this time.

Would Gerald keep his word, and could we survive the stress this move and life would put on us? We had just purchased this house in the hills of Silicon Valley, California

This house was situated on a peaceful creek side, surrounded by majestic oak trees. It had a gated entry, 2 fireplaces, separate laundry room, state-of-the art security/sound/vacuum/intercom system, marble entryway, and gourmet kitchen with greenhouse windows, huge master bedroom, with cathedral ceiling and sauna, an auto-sprinkler system with 1-hour firewalls. The master suite had its own private bath and lanai.

Gerald and I had been married for 9 years. We didn't have children but we had been talking about a family since our reconciliation. Gerald was a good provider and basically good person, however, he did have a drinking problem, and when he drank, he became physically abusive.

He owned his own company and did very well. His business was highly stressful.

Gerald used to be a New York City detective, but he hated the bureaucracy involved with all the different agencies, so he opened his own private security firm. He had 125 employees on the payroll.

I worked for a legal defense corporation. I'd been with this company for 8 years and very proud of the work we did. I did a lot of legal research for cases that involved civil rights violations.

I'm Nicole Adams, a 34-year-old, tall, hair-braided, 145-pound determined-to-stay-married Black woman.

Little did I know that my American dream would turn into a journey of nightmares and cause me to doubt all I ever strived for and believed in.

It had been a long, long day and we were so very tired from all the moving. I told Gerald, if I ever have to leave you again, it'd be for good. Life is funny, one never knows which way the wind would blow with each passing day, nor did you really consider how you would deal with the problem until it presented itself to you.

We went to the nearest Mickey D's place and ordered all food to go, so we could eat in our new home. We were so excited about our new start in our marriage and the future. We wouldn't make the same mistakes this time around. Or would we? Only time and life knew the answer.

Monday morning back at work, after being off for a couple of weeks trying to get my personal life on track. I couldn't seem to keep my mind on the job. I needed to stop at the department store and pick-up some things for the house. I thought I would leave early today to do that.

The department store was busy as usual. I finally got to the cashier and paid the bill. I had so much I had to get the car and drive around to the pick-up area so they could load the things in the car. I popped the trunk to the Jaguar and this deliveryman loaded everything in the car. I said thanks and put the car in gear to drive away.

I looked up and this man was standing at the window on the driver's side of my car. I froze. I had a large sum of cash on me, because I hadn't gone to the bank to make a deposit. Was this guy here to rob me? What did he want? I cracked the window just a fraction.

"What is it?" I asked.

This guy was really good-looking. I looked at him and knew he wasn't there to rob me or do any harm. Time stopped. Everything came to a standstill. Time became abstract and this man became the essence of the space.

The guy said he saw me walking out of the store and waited to see if I was with anyone. After seeing that I was alone, he decided to come to the car and talk to me.

"What's your name?" he asked.

"It's Nicole."

"Are you married?"

"Yes. As a matter of fact, my husband and I just went back together after being separated for a period of time."

I didn't know why I started blabbing to this stranger. He finally told me his name was Montel Bradshaw.

"Would you like to have a drink with me?" he asked.

"No, I don't think so, I don't know you". What did I look like going off with a total stranger I thought?

"You pick the place," he said. "Some place you're comfortable with."

Looking at this man, I couldn't take my eyes off of him. What did he have that was so hypnotizing? What was I doing, agreeing to go with this man? I had a husband who I just got back with. Was I willing to lose everything for a fling?

Get a grip, Nicole. I thought. You are only going to have a drink with this person, not spend the rest of your life with him.

"OK," I said. "Let's go."

We went to a place in the mall I was familiar with. We talked like old friends who had known each other for years. I found out he was married with two kids.

"A marriage made in hell," he said.

We had a few drinks and exchanged phone numbers. The time flew by and I needed to get home and start dinner. We agreed the time we spent together was nice but it was just something that happened and nothing would or could come of it. Our lives were much too complex as it was. We agreed to get on with our perspective lives and we would talk from time to time. Now my mind was saying this but in my heart something had happened. I wasn't sure what but my emotions were on overload and if I didn't get a handle I knew I was destined for deep trouble.

I got home and couldn't wait to call my best friend Sheila. Sheila I had known since childhood. We went to high school and college together. We actually met at church and became friends. We used to sing in the choir and had been friends for years. After all our togetherness, we ended up marrying guys who didn't like each other very much, so they forbade us to see each other. Can you imagine? A grown man telling a grown woman who you could have as a friend? We agreed with each of our husbands to their face that we'd no longer have a friendship, if that would make them happy. Give me a break.

Sheila and I had lunch or dinner every Saturday to stay in touch with each other. Sheila only lived a few miles away, so we went to each other's house when our husbands were gone. It wasn't our fault they didn't like each other.

I called her on the phone and started talking about this guy I met in the parking lot of the mall.

"What's he like?" she asked.

I told her he was tall, dark, and all that in every sense of the description.

"What are you going to do with him?"

"I don't know." Just as the conversation got interesting, I heard the garage door go up, and I knew Gerald was home.

"Got to go." My husband is home, and who knows what frame of mind he'll be in. I hadn't made dinner yet. I hadn't even taken my bags out of the car; I was so excited about Montel Bradshaw.

"See you Saturday at the restaurant," I said to Sheila. I hung up the phone.

Gerald met me in the hall. He stopped long enough to press me against the wall and kiss me hello. We exchanged hellos and I went into the garage to get the packages.

"How was work?" He asked.

"All right," I replied. "I took the afternoon off."

"I know you did, I called. Your secretary said you'd left for the day. Where'd you stay all afternoon"?

"Shopping." I said.

"Nicole, why do you insist on constantly spending money for this house?"

"Because we need things in it to make it comfortable."

What do you think? Look around this house is big; it needs all kinds of stuff. I thought.

I felt the tension start to engulf the whole house. I could tell Gerald was looking to start an argument, but I was in too good a mood to fall for that set-up.

"What do you want for dinner?" I asked.

"Anything you make is fine with me." Gerald said.

I walked in the kitchen and thought a nice, chilled glass of wine sounded like a plan. I put a wine glass in the freezer and went to the cellar to find a good bottle of wine. I settled on a Zinfandel.

While waiting for the glass to chill, I walked outside to look at the gardener's handiwork in the yard. The landscaping was beautiful. My flower garden was almost in full bloom. I sat down in the lounge chair and began to daydream, the telephone rang. I got up to answer it, and it was for Gerald. I called him to the phone, and he picked up the extension in the family room. I heard him asking a lot of questions and letting loose a string of profanity. I heard him slam down the phone and came outside to inform me that some major problem was going on at work. It required his presence.

"See you later, I'll have something to eat when I get back." He said.

"OK," I replied.

I heard the garage door go up. As he pulled into the street one could hear the tires of Gerald's BMW screech, as he made the corner. One of these days he's going to flip that car over. I thought.

I started to prepare dinner and had a glass of wine.

It was 9:00PM, and Gerald came in the house with the smell of booze on his breath so I hoped he had his dinner and would go to sleep.

"Hello, Nicole."

"Hello hon, did you take care of everything?" I inquired.

He stated he handled everything and asked me to fix a plate for him. He had his dinner in the dining room with a glass of wine. I ran a bath and went in the kitchen to pour a glass of wine to take in with me. Gerald asked if he could take a bath with me.

I thought, damn, can't even take a bath by myself. I said, "OK, come on." In the meantime, I made the water hotter than he liked it, so he would stay out.

He came in the bathroom and stuck his hand in the water to test the temperature. He said,

"Why did you make the water so hot?"

I wanted to say to keep you out, but I said, "Because that's how I liked it, you knew that."

He said that water would give him second-degree burns. I laughed.

"No it won't," I said.

He changed his mind and went into the living room to watch TV. Thank God! Free to bathe alone.

The workweek was almost over. I sat at the computer trying to get a report done by 3:00, so I could leave early. Montel called earlier in the week. The conversation between us was interesting. He asked if I was happily married? I refused that answer. Why? Was I happy, or did I just not want to tell this stranger all my business? He seemed to have no trouble sharing his miserable, married life with me. He told me I was a good listener.

The time was 2:45, so my watch said. My hours were 7:45 to 4:30. Since I was pretty much my own manager, I had yet to work those hours. Most times, I came in before 7:00, so I always left early.

My phone rang and my secretary told me it was a Mr. Bradshaw. My heart started to beat real fast. Calm down girl, I told myself.

"Hello, this is Nicole Adams."

"Sweet thing, this is Montel, how are you?"

I could hardly contain myself, I was falling in love with this man and there was nothing I could do to stop it.

"I'm doing fine Montel."

"Can we get together today," he asked.

I wanted to, but I knew Gerald and I made plans to go out of town for the weekend.

"I'm going out of town, I can't."

"Where are you going?"

"To Disneyland."

"I hope you have a good time. Call me anytime next week. I want to make plans for us to get together and soon." Montel said.

"Alright Montel, I will. It was nice to hear from you and I will call you." I heard the phone disconnect.

Gerald and I argued halfway down interstate 5. Why were we arguing? I didn't have a clue. I just tuned him out and started thinking about how and why we hooked up in the first place. Yes I was attracted to him when we first met. He was handsome, confident and had a lot going on at the time. We had lots of fun dating and going out and we seemed to want the same things out of life so it seemed natural to get married and strive to make our dreams come true as a couple.

Gerald after a while seemed to think he could treat me like his dad treated his mom. No way! Gerald's dad beat his mom whenever he thought she got out of line so I found out over time. She took that kind of abuse until she finally got tired and left him.

I never saw my parents abuse each other. My mom would not have tolerated that kind of behavior from my dad and she taught me the same thing. If my dad had known Gerald was abusing me in any way he would have beat Gerald down for sure.

I could see the top of the Disneyland castle. We were finally there. We went and found a hotel. Gerald complained the rates were too high. What did it matter, its not like we couldn't afford it. Gerald always tripped about the price of things for some reason. We both worked and earned a good living. Money was not one of our problems.

He never complained when it came to his family. Those vultures were always in a feeding frenzy. They didn't like me and the feeling was mutual. Most of them lived out-of-state so it wasn't too much of a problem having to deal with them. But whenever we did, they always needed something or another. They were the most needy people I'd ever known.

I suggested a hotel I stayed at when I was in Las Angeles on business. Gerald agreed. The room was nice. King-size bed, sauna, sunny deck, black bottom pool, bath with Jacuzzi, carpet so thick your feet sank down in it. We unpacked and headed for Disneyland.

We tried to ride all the popular rides, but Gerald decided he wanted to go back to the hotel and just chill out. I wanted to go for a swim and take a hot shower as well. We went back to the hotel and showered. Gerald decided he would get in the shower with me. I let him. He took the soap and lathered my body. We were all over each other. Times like these made life with Gerald worth fighting for. He could be a passionate and gentle lover as long as he was sober. After our shower we lay on the bed in each other's arms and made promises that would never be kept. We fell asleep in the essence of having the sexual need satisfied.

Gerald woke me up by kissing me on the neck. I could feel his breath on the back of my neck and my body started to respond to him.

"Are we having room service bring dinner or what?" Gerald asked.

I started to return his kiss but decided dinner might be a better idea. I got up and looked at Gerald, remembering what a wonderful time we had less than 3 hours ago.

The loving Gerald was gone and this one had come in his place. Gerald could click on you at anytime and there wasn't always a warning.

"Let's go to the hotel and eat," I said.

We got dressed and went to the dining room. The food was not bad. After dinner, we went in the hotel lounge where they had a piano bar. I got this sick feeling in my stomach, because I knew Gerald was going to drink too much and start a bunch of crap.

The guy at the piano was very good, and I felt his eyes on me. Gerald saw this guy eyeing me and gave me his twisted face look. I had a flashback of one of Gerald's violent outbursts. He had had a few drinks and it wouldn't take much to set him off. I excused myself and went back to the room to watch TV or get in the sauna, anything not to set him off.

Around 1:00AM Gerald came back to the room, boozed to the max. He got in the bed and pulled me against him. I pretended I was asleep to avoid the sloppy sex act. He mumbled something I didn't understand and fell asleep. My mind was in a thousand different places at once, but mostly it was on Montel.

I woke up and found Gerald packing his suitcase. I lay there for a moment thinking about last night and wondering if I should mention it or not. I decided not to.

Just get up and get ready to hit the road.

"Good morning," I said to Gerald.

"Hey Baby, "He said like everything was normal and fine. "You'd better get up and have breakfast so we can hit the road."

I got out of bed and called room service for breakfast. They told me breakfast would take up to 30 minutes to prepare. I asked Gerald what he wanted and placed the order for both of us. I went into the bathroom to shower and got dressed before they arrived with the food.

With breakfast out of the way, we gathered up our things and got ready to hit the road for the next 7 to 8 hours of boring highway with Gerald. I started looking through my CD collection for some music. I found Four play and they started to jam. I looked over at Gerald and he gave me this chicken smile. I wondered if he had a clue about our future together. I fell asleep for about 20 minutes and realized we stopped moving. I looked around trying to get my bearings and saw that Gerald had stopped to use the restroom at a rest stop.

I asked if he wanted to take a break and let me drive the rest of the way.

He said, "Sure, go ahead."

I didn't like the way he drove my Jag anyway. We would've taken his car but he had to have it serviced again, because he drove it like a maniac. We headed back to the interstate and continued home. I decided to play an oldie CD by the Temptations. *"Get Ready"* No matter what, their music always sounded good.

We pulled in the driveway and I touched the garage door opener. Gerald got out of the car and took the luggage in the house. I followed him and went into the bedroom to unpack. The phone rang.

"Hello," Gerald said.

They hung up on him. I knew it was probably Sheila. I hated playing these silly games but I did whatever it took. Gerald decided to go to his office and see how things were going. He asked if I wanted to come along.

I said, "No I had some things I needed to do."

He left.

I called Sheila and told her about the Disneyland event. She said she and her friend were leaving for 3 days in the Caribbean for a vacation. We talked for a while about this new guy she was going out with and where the relationship might be headed.

I called my mom to see how she was doing, and chatted for a while, and I got a call waiting beep. It was Gerald. I looked at the clock and it was now 11:00PM. I told my mom I'd call her back tomorrow. I clicked Gerald back. Gerald said the police stopped him for drunk driving.

I asked, "What do you want me to do?"

"Come down and pay the bail." Then he said, "No, never mind they'll let me out on O.R. in a few hours".

"Stay by the phone and I'll call you to come pick me up."

It was now 11:15PM. I'm so fed up with Gerald and this drunk driving. This was just like old times. He promised me this wouldn't happen this time around.

I dug through my purse and found Montel's phone number. Punched it in the phone.

He answered on the second ring. "Hello, computer room."

"Montel, this is Nicole."

"Hello pretty lady, I was starting to think you would never call, How's things"?

"OK, I guess, just thought I'd give you a call to say hello."

"Nicole, can I see you soon for lunch or something?"

"How soon, Montel?"

"Tomorrow baby, name the place and I'll be there."

I couldn't say anything for a moment. I knew within the depths of my soul that this was going to be an intense situation if I allowed myself to become involved with this man. I knew if I followed these emotions, I was in big trouble.

I said, "Yes, I'll meet you at Sugar's". Sugar's was one of my favorite restaurants.

"I know where it is". "See you tomorrow at 2:00PM, be sweet." He hung up.

Montel had a smile on my face no drama could wipe off.

It was 1:30AM; I heard Gerald put the key in the door. He came in the house mad as hell. He looked at me like I was the cause of this latest mess. I didn't say anything. Gerald went in the bathroom; soon I heard the shower running. I got in bed and more flashbacks of our early days came to mind. The drinking, the fighting, the bruises, the lies and excuses. I needed some peace of mind. I fell asleep with Montel's voice in my head.

Sunday morning, I turned on the stereo to hear some gospel music to give me some inspiration to get through this day. I was nervous, because I was to meet Montel. I told Gerald I was meeting a friend. He could care less anyway. I dressed carefully, a silk jacquard jacket and matching two-tier chiffon skirt in watercolors, and a taupe platform pump. Finally a chance to wear my new white gold pendant with matching hoop earrings. I looked in the mirror and the reflection stared back at me was a soul that was happy, and excited about life and love.

It was almost scary. I felt too good.

I went into the garage and got into my car. I pulled out my lip liner and lined my lips one last time. I wanted this man to kiss me on this day. I wanted to appeal to him as much as possible.

As I was sitting there lost in fantasy. Gerald appeared and reality set in.

"What time will you be back?" He said.

"A couple of hours, I guess". "Why?" I wanted to know.

"No reason", "Have a good time."

Just like Gerald to make me feel guilty for meeting another man. I pulled out of the driveway with less heart than I originally started with. Gerald's brother was picking him up later in the day to take him to pick up his car from impound. Gerald was always spending money on impound fees or drunk driving tickets. He had the nerve to complain about me spending money on the house, and look at all the waste of his money on foolishness.

I headed for the freeway and was so nervous I could feel myself shaking. I stopped for gas and walked up to the ATM to use the card and 2 guys volunteered to pump the gas for me. I was flattered at all the attention and appreciative of the help.

I pulled into the parking lot but didn't know if Montel was there or not. He saw me and came to the car, opened the door and handed me a long stemmed red rose and then gave me a hug as I got out.

I stood there dumb-founded and breathless. He kissed me on the lips so lightly that I thought I'd faint from the touch. He looked in my eyes and told me how good I looked. His gaze made me feel he was seeing my soul. I looked at him and he was beautifully dressed. This man must spend a fortune on clothes I thought.

He asked if I was ready to go inside. I could care less about food at this point. If this man asked me for anything, I'm not sure I could say no.

We're seated in a booth that was very intimate, and he touched me under the table with his leg. I didn't move. I could feel the heat against my skin, and I looked at him and smiled. Obviously, he was feeling the same way so he reached over and held my hand and gave it a squeeze.

The waiter came around, but I was too nervous to order or eat. What was I doing here with this man? What if someone I knew saw me? Why did his touch feel so good?

Finally, I mustered enough strength to order the prawn salad. Montel ordered Champagne. I sipped my first taste, although I really wanted to guzzle it to stop my insides from shaking so much. I maintained my facade of ultimate cool. I sipped some more. He asked if the champagne was to my satisfaction. I said it was. He told me how pleased he was to spend this time with me and how he hoped this would be the beginning of something special.

I was speechless, I couldn't breathe, I couldn't see, I was totally gone. I had lost all control of my emotional self. How could his wife take him for granted so easily? What was wrong with her? He smiled at me and leaned over to kiss my lips. I didn't object.

He put his hand in my hand and held it until the food was served.

After the meal was over, he paid the bill and walked me to my car. The time passed so fast, it made me feel like I was on a whirlwind and being hurled at some super speed.

He put his arms around me and squeezed tightly. I had never felt such a sense of safety in such a dangerous position. I reached and put my arms around him and squeezed just as tight. He kissed me softly and looked into my eyes and kissed me deeper. I felt like I was falling in a deep hole and there was nothing I could do to keep my balance but hope and pray that something was down there to break my fall, so I wouldn't be hurt too badly or even worse killed from the impact.

He said, "I'll call you at work". "Take care of yourself until then."

"It was a pleasure to spend this time with you, I enjoyed it." I said.

I watched him walk to his car and as he drove past me, he put his fingers to his lips and gestured a kiss. I did it back and put my car in gear to drive away. As I hit the freeway I picked up the rose and lifted it to my nose to take in the scent and remember the man.

This was a day I would remember for a long time. I thought. Would I give up the marriage I had fought so hard to save for a married man? I had all these questions in my head and heart with no answers.

As I approached my house, the driveway was filled with cars. I blew the horn and out came Gerald's brother, Tate. I couldn't stand him. He was a thief, a con artist, and a jailbird. I ignored him and pulled into the garage. Gerald came out, drunk, as he wanted to be. He put his arm around my shoulders and kissed at me. I excused myself. They made remarks on how Gerald allowed me to go out looking good like that. Wasn't he afraid somebody might steal me away from him? I smiled to myself.

"You are on the right track". "Too bad Gerald can't see what's happening to us". I said out loud to myself.

I undressed, put on some jeans, and proceeded to the kitchen to make something to eat. I walked back to the family room and looked out the window. Everybody was gone, boy could I clear a room. I was really glad for the peace and quiet that allowed me to daydream about my afternoon.

Gerald came back in the house. He asked, "Where did you go"?

I said "Sugar's."

"What's for dinner?"

"I think I'll make stuffed chicken breasts."

He put his hand on my waist and asked, "Why are you so happy"?

"You see your boyfriend at Sugar's?"

"Yes."

"I hope you had a good time with him."

I ignored Gerald. He was trying to start an argument. I continued to make the meal and tried to hurry so I could get away from him before he said or did something to me. I felt some guilt but I could live with it.

He went outside and sat on the patio to wait for the meal to be completed.

Thank you God!

Gerald could be violent if he'd been drinking, and I'd learned not to provoke him. That was one of the reasons for our separation. He promised to seek professional help with the drinking. He did for a while and things between us got better. We had a strong marriage, so I thought. That was why I chose not to divorce him, but the drinking was starting again, when I mentioned it he said I nagged him. I wouldn't nag this time. If the violence started again, I'd just leave for good. Over the last few years, Gerald had given me a black eye, and numerous bruises, a broken arm, and lacerations. For a while, I thought my body was supposed to always, be sore and stiff.

Dinner was ready. I called Gerald to come and eat. The table was set immaculately, as always. I always tried to set a nice table no matter what kind of food we ate; it would be more appealing if it were served in a beautiful manner.

Gerald said, "I always enjoy sitting down to eat a meal you've prepared."

We completed the meal, and Gerald went into the living room to watch one of the many videos in his collection. I wondered what was going to happen to his business, if he kept going to jail for drunk driving? This time, he was lucky, because he knew someone high up in the police department that would have his arrest paperwork disappear and none would be the wiser.

The clock said 6:00AM. Gerald was still asleep. He usually didn't get up until 8:00. I made my way to the bathroom to shower and get dressed. I remembered an interview with an attorney at 8:30 this morning for an opening at the firm. I wondered what this one would be like. They were all so straitlaced, or pretended to be. The one that was due for the interview was just what the firm was looking for, except he had no personality. He was so robotic. The clientele, we dealt with, required some personable skills. This job required someone with the legal savvy as well as people skills.

My shower was done, and I stood in front of the closet trying to decide what to wear. Since today was my day to interview a prospective employee, I decided a suit was in order. I decided on a beige, double-breasted shawl collar jacket, and straight skirt, matching silk shell underneath and pearl choker. My pearl and diamond earrings would work and high-heel, black open-toed platform pumps. Not too high but just high enough.

Gerald opened his eyes as I was putting the final touches on my make-up.

"You look nice today."

"Thank you."

I gathered the rest of my papers and put them in my totebag. By now Gerald was sitting on the side of the bed staring at me.

"Nicole, I love you." "I know you find that hard to believe but I do."

My heart dropped because I knew it was just a matter of time before our marriage was over. I no longer loved Gerald, I feared him. I leaned over and kissed him on the cheek.

"Have a good day Gerald, see you later."

I arrived at work and there were 2 messages on my voice mail from Montel. I punched his number at work, and he answered.

"How are you?" Montel said.

"I'm fine."

"Yesterday was something and I been thinking about you a lot". "My wife suspects I'm seeing somebody, but she would suspect it anyway."

"Why is that"?

"Because she and I have had so many problems and there have been other women."

"Montel, I had such a good time being with you, it felt so right."

"I know baby, I felt the same way, when are we getting together again, just to talk?"

"Listen", I said.

I was interrupted by a knock on the door.

"Montel, I have to go, I have an interview scheduled and the person is here."

"Call me back so we can make plans, OK"? Montel said.

"OK." I hung up.

I thought Montel just wants to be friends with me, nothing more. Yeah Nicole, sure. Justify it anyway you like. You know exactly what time it is. As I sat there with all my tidy justifications, the interviewee knocked on the office door.

He asked for a N. Adams. I stated I was the one he was looking for.

"The only name I had was N. Adams. I expected to interview with a man."

I'm not sure if this guy was sexist or just rude and crude but I had already developed a dislike for this person.

"Have a seat," I said

We began the interview process. I interviewed him hard and heavy, to see how he dealt with the pressure. He was so angry, but he tried to contain himself. His body language told me, if he had the chance, he could knock me out of my chair with no problem. I laughed to myself. I was good at this job, that's why I had it.

This was a firm that handled civil rights violation cases. We needed attorneys who could and would be flexible, not some hotshot trying to make a name for him self. This guy thanked me for the opportunity to interview and reached to shake my hand. I learned a long time ago how not let the stronger person grab my hand first and squeeze real hard. I knew this guy had that in mind, so I just touched his hand with my fingertips and gave his hand a sturdy grip.

"Goodbye, I said and good luck."

It was past 1:00 and I had been too busy to stop and get something for lunch. I needed to type a report on the job interview and why I felt this person was not suitable for the position. I began typing and my secretary buzzed me about my husband being on the line and gave me the other phone messages for the day. I put my phone on intercom and said,

"Hello, Gerald."

He said he had been waiting for me to call him back for 2 hours.

I explained I was in a meeting all morning.

"What is so important?" I asked.

"Do you want to go out for dinner tonight?"

This could not wait until later? I wondered.

"No thanks, I'd rather cook or order takeout food. The place in the shopping center, near the house, even delivers."

"OK" he grumbled, whatever", "I'll see you later." "Bye."

"Bye."

I returned my calls and asked my secretary to confirm my reservation for an upcoming case in 2 weeks. My secretary Jason was one of the best in the business. This man could type almost 100 words-a-minute and made few, if any errors. He had a reputation in the legal world and firms would almost give up their first-born to have him. I lucked out, when I came to work for this firm, Jason was already there and he was assigned to me. Over the years he had become a good friend.

"Nicole, you need to select a car for rental, and I'll confirm for you."

"Will do." I replied.

Jason had some papers for me to sign and a few things to go over with me, which took another hour, and finally I was finished for the day.

A big case was coming up, it wasn't official but I knew I had been chosen to work on it with another attorney.

On the way home I mentally made a list of groceries to order and have the store deliver them. I hated grocery stores and so did Gerald. I would go to the fruit stand but generally avoided the supermarket like the plague.

I arrived home, got undressed and sat down in the living room. This room we never used. I tried to talk Gerald out of buying this big, expensive house. No way, he wanted it, regardless. I liked it. I just wished things were better between us so we could have babies and make use of all this room.

I decided I'd call Gerald at work and see what his earlier phone call was really all about. His secretary answered.

"Adams Security firm."

"Hello, Stacy."

"Hi Nicole, How are you?"

"Just fine, is Gerald around?"

"No, he went out on a call and hasn't come back yet. Is there a message for him?"

"No Stacy thanks, I'll see him when he gets home. Bye." I hung up the phone.

Stacy had a thing for Gerald, and I wondered if they had been together but he said she was not his type. She used to try and do everything to get him to like her but for some reason it never worked. She was so tacky. She knew we were married but still was disrespectful. I knew he had to have talked to her regarding our marriage at some point. Gerald was traditional when it came to what a man's place was; he liked to be the one to do the chasing, not the other way around. Its too bad you didn't know that Stacy. *I thought.*

I walked into the kitchen and the phone rang. It was Sheila.

"What's up girl?" she said.

"Nothing and everything." We both laughed.

"Nicole, when you use those words, anything could happen."

"Don't I know it."

"Nicole, what's going on with Montel?"

"I haven't decided yet". "He just wants to be friends". "Can you believe that?"

Sheila said, "No, I don't". "He wants you". "What does he have to offer you?"

I said, "At this point in time, I don't know". "We enjoyed each other's company. "He made me come alive." "I had forgotten there was such a thing as passion and depth."

"Be careful Nicole, this guy sounds too good to be for real."

"Sheila, there's this attraction I have for him that's so powerful, It scares me to think about it."

"Go slow my friend". "Please weigh all the options."

"I will." "Anyway so much for Montel". "How's your packing coming along for the cruise?"

"Girl," Sheila said, "I haven't even started to pack yet."

"You'd better get busy."

She laughed. "We'll talk this weekend at Sugar's." "See ya."

I hung up the phone.

I started thinking about the job offer one of the partners in my law firm offered me. I hadn't told Gerald yet.

They offered to reimburse whatever costs might incur if I wanted to attend law school. I always wanted to get a law degree. I had the expertise in a lot of different areas of the law, which had always been my problem; I never decided which area of law to choose. I realized this was a chance of a lifetime. I'd be crazy not to take advantage of this. Law school was expensive. Anyone that I could get in would cost a pretty penny.

I got the phone book and found the Chinese place that would deliver and, ordered dinner for Gerald and I. I heard Gerald's car pull in the garage.

He came in the house and said "Hi, baby, how was work?'

"It was fine today."

We exchanged pleasantries.

He asked, "Stacy said you called. What did you want?"

"Well, I was going to wait until later, but we might as well talk about it now."

"Are you pregnant?"

"No."

"What is it?"

"Gerald this isn't working between us. You're drinking again, and I can't stand it."

"What do you want from me, Nicole?" he yelled.

He went into the kitchen and looked for a bottle of wine. There was none. He come down the hall in a rage and almost knocked me down, as I met him head on. He looked at me and I saw his eyes. I also smelled the liquor. He was so outraged. I was too slow in reading what his action might be. He grabbed me by the arm and pushed me so hard against the corner of the wall, I saw black.

When I woke up I saw these people with white clothes on, and they asked me how I felt. I was disoriented for a moment and wondered where I was. I said I had a headache. They told me they put 7 stitches in my head to close the wound, but I'd be fine. They wanted to keep me overnight for observation.

I lay there thinking, this was happening again. A new town, different hospital, same old reason. I reached for the phone to call Sheila.

She picked up the phone on the first ring.

"Nicole, are you all right?" She was talking so much she didn't give me a chance to say much. Finally, she allowed me to tell her what happened.

"Sheila, listen." "This is finally it". "I'm going to leave Gerald for good this time". "He is never going to get to hurt me again." The doctor said I have to stay here overnight, and then I can go home. "

"I've got to find me a new home. Gerald and I have been in that house less than 1 year and now I've got to move. I can't live in that house with that manic."

"Sheila, come by here tomorrow, I need you to do some things for me."

"OK." she said. "Do you need anything right now?"

I looked around the hospital room and saw my clothes I had on when they brought me here, they were full of blood. Tears streamed down my face.

Sheila yelled in the telephone, "Nicole, what is it?"

"Nothing, I'll be fine."

"I'm coming down there right now. What hospital are you in?"

"Masters General." I replied and hung up the phone.

Gerald sneaked into the room.

"Why are you here?"

"I'm sorry Nicole, I didn't mean for this to happen again to us."

"Yes, you're always sorry after the fact. Why aren't you in jail or dead or something? Get out of here! The sight of you makes me sick. I should have never taken you back. You drink, you lie, you cheat, and you think I don't know about the fling you had with that skeezer Charmaine!!"

The pupils in his eyes become the size of quarters. He looked like he might cry for a moment, but my rage was beyond giving him any sympathy at this point.

"I'm through with you. Get out!"

"Tomorrow, when they release me, I'm moving out! You will cause no more pain and beatings on me!"

The doctor rushed in and told Gerald to leave; when the door opened I could see a couple of policeman standing in the hallway. Gerald left.

The doctor told me charges should be pressed against Gerald for abusing me. I asked the doctor to leave me alone because I was not feeling well. He agreed and said he'd come back a little later.

I started to cry again. Crying was not going to get me out of this situation. I needed to take some action and control of my life.

I called my boss and explained I'd had an accident and would be off the rest of the week, maybe longer, but would be able to work at home

Luckily, I had no more interviews scheduled for the week. The company set up a computer system in my house, so that would work out great.

I called Susan Overfelt, a Realtor I knew and told her I needed a place to Live. I just needed a safe place of my own. She asked what I was looking for and I told her a condo or small house would work just fine. The priority was I needed it now.

She said, "I'll call you in a few days."

"OK, but call on my cell phone, not my home number." I hung up.

The doctor came back in the room. He had a police officer with him and the police officer said he needed to ask me some questions about what happened to me. They went on to explain how vital it was to file a report so criminal charges could be filed against Gerald. I knew these things! I answered all the questions and a warrant would be issued for Gerald's arrest for spousal abuse. What purpose would it serve to have that fool in jail? They would arrest him and he would be out in time to help me move out of the house. He had a business to run. I had a life to get back on track.

I told the doctor I would not file charges, I explained Gerald was sick and needed professional help not jail time. They looked at me like I just blew in from Mars.

The doctor said, "Ms. Adams, I know you have your own personal reasons for not filing charges, but please do something to avoid this kind of situation from happening again, for your safety!"

"I will."

They left the room.

Sheila arrived.

"Nicole, are you all right?" She hugged me.

"I'm all right. As a matter of fact, I feel better than I've felt in a long time. Maybe it took a knock on the head to make me see Gerald for what he really is, and understand I can't make him be well on my own."

Sheila stood there looking at me and started to cry.

"Nicole, why did you stay with him?" "Do you love him?" "What is it?"

"Stop crying Sheila", I said. "I'm the one that should cry, for being so stupid to put up with this madness."

"You know I cry at the thought of anything happening to you". "The sight of you here with that bandage on your head due to Gerald, should be a wake-up call for you to leave that crazy man"

I felt bad for Sheila; I realized at that moment that other's hurt when I hurt. My mother suspected Gerald was hitting me but never confronted me about it and I never told her.

"Sheila, do you realize, I don't even have a change of clothes, fresh underwear, nothing?"

"No problem, my friend, I'll go buy whatever you need right now."

"Sheila, I don't have my wallet or credit cards, no I.D. "

"Do you want me to go by your house and get them from Gerald?"

"Who got hit on the head? You or me? Gerald hates the sight of you! He would not give them to you. I'll call him tonight and have him bring something in the morning."

"Nicole, do you have a death wish? Hello! Is he not the cause of your being here in the first place?"

"Look, I know Gerald, he won't hit me again, at least not tomorrow. Go home, get some rest, I'll call you as soon as I get my plan in place."

"I can't believe you're going back to him!" Sheila shouted.

"I know you don't understand. I have to do, what I have to do, whether it makes sense to you or not."

"Nicole, you know I'd do anything for you. You've always been there for me. Remember when I was married to that low-lifed husband of mine, and you did the divorce for me."

"Yes," I said.

"The legal work you did for me was pure genius. The lawyer that represented me in court, without your expertise wouldn't have handled the case as well."

"Sheila, in your case, we lucked out, because I was able to find assets he was hiding from you and all kinds of business dealings he was into that was community property."

"I got everything I asked for in the divorce and that set me and the kids financially, for life. Thanks to you."

"Hey, I just did my job."

Sheila stood there looking at me with tears in her eyes. I don't know what she was thinking but whatever it was she decided to keep it to her self.

"I'll see you tomorrow." Sheila said.

This was the moment I dreaded. Alone with the harsh reality of dealing with what happened to me again. I needed to call Gerald to bring me some clothes and my purse. Might as well get it over with. I punched in the telephone number.

"Hello," Gerald said.

His voice sounded like he was expecting me to call. He probably was. Our behavior was almost predictable if it hadn't been so pathetic.

"Gerald it's me, Nicole."

"How are you?"

"Let's not do small talk, I need you to bring me some clothes and my purse."

"I'm on my way right now"

"No, in the morning about 9:00 would be good." I broke the connection.

At this point I hated Gerald, hated what I had allowed him to do to me for the past 7 years, hated the fact, I was too cowardly to do something about it. Hated the fact that I always went back to him.

I woke up the next morning with a terrible headache. I got up to use the bathroom and felt dizzy. I sat down on the side of the bed and the doctor came into the room with a bag that looked familiar.

"Good morning Nicole, how are you feeling?"

I explained about the headache and dizziness.

"It will pass after a couple of days, stated the doctor. If not give me a call and we'll get you back in here.

"Please take care of yourself. By the way, your husband is waiting outside for you."

He gave me an odd look and walked out of the room.

Gerald came in the room and told me he would be parked at the hospital entrance.

Finally, I was dressed, and the nurse asked if I was ready to go.

Yes I was as ready as I would ever be.

She had a wheelchair she insisted I take advantage of. Rather than argue with her I sat down and she wheeled me outside to the entrance where my husband was waiting to take me home. When we reached the outside, Gerald opened the car door, and before, I got into the car, I noticed a dent on the side of the car. Gerald knew I saw it, but said nothing about it, and neither did I. I got in the car, and he pulled off.

As we drove, I wondered if he would mention this dent. I didn't bring it up for fear of a fight. That was something else I needed to change. Our car insurance policy was together. I needed to call the agent and have me taken off and put on my own. The premium was already so high it was unreal. I drove a luxury car, but my driving record was nothing like Gerald's, so the premium would go down.

Gerald pulled into the driveway and got out of the car to open the door for me. He took my tote bag and opened the front door.

As soon as I entered the living room, the smell of stale cigarettes hit my nose. I opened the patio door and the living room windows to air out the house. As I looked out the window, Gerald was talking to the neighbor. He saw me at the window and waved. I turned from the window and walked down the hall to my bedroom to unpack and get settled in.

Gerald came in the room and stated he was going to work. I didn't say anything to him.

He said, "Nicole, I know you're going to leave me for good this time. I won't give up the house and furniture without a fight."

I couldn't believe he was saying this to me. I was shocked he even bothered to think that far ahead. I knew he had talked to his family and they put this take all you can get from Nicole in his head.

They had totally forgotten, that I'm the one that helped Gerald build his business. I worked full-time at the law firm and almost full-time for Gerald in the evening in the early years of his business.

I started to say something, but my mind said, save it. This is not the battle to pick.

"Gerald, just go on. I think you have done enough damage to me for one lifetime. Don't you?"

"Yeah, I'll go, but did you hear what I said."

"Yes, I heard you." Should I trade insults back and forth with this fool or just hold my peace and deal with him later. I chose the later. Gerald slammed the front door on his way out.

This time I was taking no chances with him. I walked out into the garage and looked in my car to get the snub-nosed 38 my brother gave me last Christmas. I kept it in the glove compartment. I had a permit for it. I reminisced about the conversation my brother and I had a few months ago.

Nicole, he said, I hope you never have to use it, but if you need protection from that stupid husband of yours, here it is. Please take care of yourself. Why don't you leave that jerk? You can do better than him. I can't make you leave him, but I can help you protect yourself against him.

As I stood in the garage with the feel of the cold steel in my hand, thinking about the conversation my brother and I had. I heard the phone ring.

"Hello."

"Hi Nicole, it's Chantal Perkins." Chantal was my boss at the law firm.

"Hi," I replied back.

"Listen Nicole, I need you to fly to Los Angeles for 2 or 3 days next week. Will you be up to it by then?"

Here was the official notification about that case. I was being brought in to work on it.

"Yes. I'm fine now."

"What happened?" she asked.

"Just a little accident."

"Nicole?"

"Yes, Chantal."

"You know you can talk to me if there's a problem."

"Look, Chantal, Gerald is drinking again, and the violence has started. I'm in the process of looking for a place to live and get on my feet."

Chantal said, "Get out of there before something happens that you'll regret."

Chantal stayed in a marriage and was beaten for 10 years by her husband. One day, she got tired of the beatings and shot him dead, but not before he had beaten their 10-year-old daughter to death. Chantal wasn't charged for his death since it was self-defense. She was a family law specialist and went around the country giving seminars about domestic violence. She's also a children's advocate in the Social Services department. This was her way of dealing with the death of her child by trying to help others protect theirs.

"Nicole, you know how I feel about you and that situation." "What do you plan to do?"

"I am looking for a place to live."

"Look, you can come and live at my house if that's what's keeping you there with that madman."

"Thank you, but I will be all right until I can get moved."

"Nicole, Gregory Taylor has a case that you briefed a few weeks ago. I know you have heard all the hoopla in the media about this case."

"I also know you were expecting to be brought in on it too. I need you to go to court with him and do the research. With your expertise, we can win it. When are you going back to school to get that law degree, so you can handle these cases yourself? You know just as much, if not more than most of these ivy-leagued, pinstriped, macho men."

"Thanks Chantal, for the vote of confidence. I promised you and myself that, when I got out of this mess, that would be the first thing I did."

"I'm going to make sure of it." said Chantal. "Look, I'll send over the paperwork by messenger this afternoon. It's too much to fax, otherwise, I'd do that. You brief everything by tomorrow, and Greg will be in touch with you sometime after that."

"Nicole, I'm counting on you guys to win this case. It's worth 3 million dollars to the firm. Of course your pay won't be monopoly money, either. Plus the publicity involved is all politics so this alone could make a great career move for both of you. I'll be in touch". "Bye."

"Bye," I said.

I went to the closet and took down a suitcase for my upcoming trip. I wondered if I should call Montel and tell him what was going on. I decided to call. I punched the number, and he answered on the first ring.

"Where have you been?" he asked.

"I've been trying to stay alive."

"I called you 5 or 6 times but you didn't return any of my calls." "What do you mean, trying to stay alive?" "Is something wrong?"

I don't want to go into a lot of detail on the phone right now, cause I don't want Gerald to walk in on me. My trying to explain to Montel in 10 words or less won't work. So I'll just put him off until I can really talk.

"Look, Montel, my reason for calling is to tell you I'll be out of town for a few days."

"Nicole, I really need to see you. I need to talk to you."

"Montel, I'll call you when I finish taking care of this business at hand. Take care of yourself."

I hung up the phone. I should tell him what's going on, but I couldn't bring myself to do that just yet. I didn't want to become too

dependent on him to get me through this. I needed time to get myself together. My head was so jacked-up I didn't know if I was coming or going.

My pager went off, letting me know I had a call on my cell phone. I found the cell phone in the bottom of my purse. It was the Realtor.

"Hi," I said to her.

"Nicole, I found a place you might like. When can you come over to my office?"

"I can come right now." I said.

I arrived at the Realtor's office and we drove about 45 minutes seemed like, into the countryside.

We parked in the parking lot of this beautifully landscaped property. We walked across this lawn that looked like green carpeting, with gardens of beautiful roses, just starting to bloom. We walked up a stairwell to a double-door entry. She unlocked the door and the entryway had three-stairs leading down into a large living room. I walked over to the patio and looked out, over the swimming pool, above the pool were the mountains. The view was breathless. I went into the kitchen and could tell it had been remodeled and had high-tech appliances.

I noticed the rock fireplace and wet bar, the master bedroom had a vaulted ceiling and opened to a redwood deck. This place would be perfect to start all over in. It was bright, airy and had an aura of peace and tranquility. I had to get that peace within my self and then I could go on with my life. I hadn't had peace in a long time. This time around, me and peace were going to have a long relationship.

The Realtor decided to leave me alone, and let me decide what I wanted to do. I allowed myself to feel, and dream, and have hopes for a better future. I almost started to cry. I realized my next move would be a permanent one and would change my life. I owed myself the chance to live a life without being beat down or hit.

As I prepared to let the Realtor know my decision, I began to feel better about myself. I knew she had several other places but I liked this one. This would be the last time I moved. I continued on to the office and signed the necessary paperwork to begin the process for purchase. I told Susan I needed the place quickly. I wrote a check for the necessary amount and closed the deal. Since the place was empty. I could move in like a renter until escrow closed. It was nice to have ties with people that made life simpler.

"It was a pleasure doing business with you Ms. Adams," said Susan.

I laughed to myself. I guess it was. I just gave you a check for $35,000.00. I would say that to my customer too. Thank God I had saved a nice nest egg for emergencies. Gerald was insane if he thought he would walk away with everything from that house. I worked to help make that purchase too. I bet his memory got real short regarding how much money I contributed to making that purchase.

I arrived back at the house and went straight to the closet, and began to pack my clothes and other necessary things. I decided to take a break from the clothes after 3 trips to the car to load them. I found a hefty trash bag and put shoeboxes in them. I was going to wait and try to talk to Gerald, first, but I knew that wouldn't work.

I began to box up my computer and fax machine, and files. While I was boxing up this stuff, I called the phone company to get service.

The phone company said in 2 working days, they could have everything up and running.

My heart was beating so fast, I though I might start to hyperventilate at any second. I put this stuff on the front seat. Lucky for me, I was well organized, or this move could take hours.

As I entered the house again, the phone rang. I answered and it was Sheila. I told her I found a place to live and she asked if I had told Gerald, yet. I told her he wasn't at home and I was trying to leave before he got there. She asked if I wanted her to come over.

I said, No. I could handle it but if she didn't hear from me in a couple of hours, come over with the National Guard. As I said National Guard I remembered the 38 my brother gave me for protection.

"Nicole this is for you," he said. "I wish you would leave that silly fool, you deserve better than him. I can't protect you from him but this cold, blue piece of steel can."

I heard somebody calling my name and remembered I was talking to Sheila on the phone.

"I'm sorry," I said to her. "I was tripping on something my brother said to me."

"Nicole give me the new address and I'll come and help you get settled in. I gave her the new address but told her to go there and wait. We hung up, and I continued to pack.

I heard Gerald come into the house. He didn't park his car in the garage. He walked to the bedroom and saw all my suitcases on the floor.

"He said, "Well you tramp I knew you'd pull this. This is how you always deal with your problems. You run away like a child."

I smelled the liquor, so I knew not to antagonize him. The least thing I said would set him off. He surprised me and left to use the bathroom in the hallway.

I reached for the gun and put it in reach in case I had to use it. I slipped the safety off and let a bullet slide into the chamber. If I had to use it, then so be it.

Good thing I had some shooting lessons and continued to go to the range once a week.

Gerald come back in the room and didn't say anything. Just looked at me with a hard gaze that sent chills through my body. I

28

could tell the alcohol had taken over any reasoning with him. I was standing over a dresser drawer, taking all my lingerie out of the drawer putting them into a suitcase. He came over and held up this teddie that he claimed he never saw before.

"Did one of your lawyer men buy this for you?" I wanted to say yes, but he was not in any mood for me to be playing game show contestant with. Any wrong answer would set him off and I would have to shoot him or if he got the ups on me I knew he would hurt me this time for sure.

"No," I said. You bought it last year for Valentine's Day."

"Yeah, I bet I did."

I grabbed everything in that drawer, stuffed it in the suitcase, and zipped it up. I had emptied 4 drawers and had 2 to go. My bra drawer was next. Why didn't I empty that one first? I needed bras more than skimpy nighties.

Gerald pushed me back on the bed and started to take my top off. He ripped the buttons off and attempted to take my bra off. He succeeded. I was scared almost out of my mind, because if I didn't submit, he would beat the hell out of me and I would have no choice but to shoot him dead. No way would the police be here in time to keep him from doing some serious damage to me. It was easier to submit. He took his hands and put them on both of my breasts and began to fondle them.

He pinned me on the bed and was on top of me. I couldn't really move away from him. He tried to kiss me, and the smell of alcohol made me want to gag. He started to kiss my neck and breasts. The doorbell rang. He continued and who ever was ringing the doorbell leaned on it for all it was worth.

Thank you, whoever you are, for coming, I thought. I got up and got a shirt to cover myself and Gerald went to the bathroom. I opened the door and there stood Sheila looking like an angel. I hugged her.

She screamed, "What's wrong?"

I started to cry and she told me she was calling the police. I told her no.

"I'm all right. "Wait outside for me."

Gerald shouted from the hallway, "What, does that witch want?"

"Why doesn't she get on her broom and fly away"?

I told Sheila, "Get in your car and pull around the corner, I'll meet you in 15 minutes." She left.

"Nicole, we need to talk." Gerald said.

"I know we do, but you're drunk and you just tried to rape me."

"Rape you. B——, you need to read some more law books. How could I rape you?"

"We're not getting anywhere. I'll come back tomorrow to get the rest of my things and try and talk to you about some kind of settlement."

"Nicole, you must be crazy if you think I'm letting you take everything from my house. This is all mine."

I couldn't believe Gerald had gone this far.

"Look you jerk." I said. "I don't want everything." "I want the living room furniture, the kitchen stuff, the rest of my personal stuff, and the rest you can stick up your drunk butt. I am so sick of you I could just scream. Your drinking, name-calling, and your sick, selfish, insecure ways, and last but not least, your total disrespect for me." "I've had it with you. This time, no matter what you say, I won't come back. Get a good lawyer. I'm going to fight you with everything I know. If you bust up this stuff, before I can come back and get it, I'll take you to court and sue you for everything but the drawers you have on your butt."

I walked to my car and felt pretty useless and alone, but alive, unhurt and soon to be on my own. I gained a new attitude. I would no longer be a victim in my own marriage and home. Those days had ended. I pulled around the corner and saw Sheila on her cell phone. She saw me and hung up.

I pulled beside her and told her to follow me. I called her on her cell phone and told her all that happened while we drove to the new address.

We arrived at the house and started to unpack. I set up the computer and fax machine in one of the spare bedrooms, I would use as an office. It dawned on me; I didn't have a bed, blanket or any of that stuff.

Sheila must have read my mind.

She said, "Nicole, I have the kid's sleeping bags in the trunk of the car from their last sleep over. I never took them out of the car. You can use them for as long as you need to."

30

"OK"

I started to cry and felt sorry for myself. This voice in my head said. What are you crying for? You could be like so many unfortunate women and have to stay with a dog for a husband and take his mess. But you are blessed; you have a good job with a very bright future, money in the bank, and financial security. Get a grip, and move on. Well that was a wake up call.

I continued to put away what I could. I realized I hadn't eaten all day. I'm sure Sheila was starved as well.

I called a restaurant that delivered and ordered some food. As I waited for the food to be delivered, I called Montel. They said he had the next two nights off. I should've known. They are never there when you needed them.

Sheila came in with more clothes and put them away for me. I told her I ordered some food and it would be here shortly.

"I don't know how to thank you," I said to her.

"Just stay away from Gerald will be thanks enough, that fool is crazy."

Gerald was a sad human being. I lost my appetite thinking about him.

"Sheila, when we first met, I didn't know he drank like a fish and would get drunk and be violent and crazy. I met him when he was a rookie cop. He had been a cop for about 2 years and looked good in that uniform. We started to date, and found we got along well with each other. He had a jacked up childhood and issues but he wanted to do something with himself and he had a determination I hadn't seen in most of the men I had dated in the past. So he moved into my apartment with me. Nine months later, we were married. We had the same dreams and goals back then. He never appeared insecure about me going to school or trying to better myself in anyway up until I got the first promotion at work. I knew he mentioned he wanted a wife to be there for him, but I wasn't aware, until later that he was insecure about me or my job."

"Gerald was tired of the crap he had to endure at the precinct, so he quit the force and decided to open his own security firm. A Black man with a vision is what he called himself. We started from scratch. I did all the accounting, secretarial work, and anything else he needed until he got established. His company was one of very few where the security was trained on the premises in firearm safety and use. He had come a long way with the business. I hated to see him lose it because of his drinking."

"You know Nicole," said Sheila. "I have better insight into the kind of person Gerald really was after listening to you talk about him. But that doesn't excuse him for abusing you. You'd think that jerk would be more appreciative of what he's had, instead of acting like a fool."

I looked at the clock and it was 3:00AM. I told Sheila we needed to get some sleep. I was exhausted after my nightmare of a day.

"Hey Sheila, I really appreciate you staying with me tonight. What would I do without you in my life?"

She laughed and said, "I hope you never have to find out."

"I hope I don't either." We've been talking about me all night. I forgot to ask how your plans for the cruise are going?"

"Girl they are coming along. My friend Julian is going with me."

"Julian, the guy, you brought to my office party, who is ten years younger than you?"

"That's the one."

" Go girl. This should be a cruise you won't ever forget. I bet the sex will be so hot, they'll have to bring a water hose and goggles to your cabin every day to cool down the temperature and steam in the room."

"On that note." said Sheila as she laughed, I'm going to sleep. Goodnight."

"Goodnight." I said.

A new day arrived. I didn't sleep well at all, what little sleeping I did. I woke up and remembered where I was. I didn't sleep well in strange places. That was why I preferred my own bed. Speaking of bed, I didn't have one. I needed to go to the factory outlet or someplace and get one. I needed to get a lot of things. I called Gerald. Gerald didn't answer. I would get dressed and try to contact him later.

I phoned the office and gave Jason my new address. I gave instructions on how to contact me and let them know I'd be working at home.

Sheila got up and cursed to herself about the hard floor. She started to light a cigarette and remembered I didn't smoke and my "No Smoking" rule in my house. This one time, I made an exception and told her it was OK as long as she did it in the kitchen with the window and door open. She decided to wait, because the morning air was cold. She washed up as best she could and got dressed and left for her daily tasks. She was financially set with her two children. She traveled and did volunteer work to take up her time. *Must be nice, I thought to myself.*

I went into the master bedroom and found the suitcase with a blouse and a pair of slacks. Fortunately, I pulled those things out of the closet, with hangers on them, so all I had to do was hang them back in the closet. I put away all I could until later in the day. I got in the car and started to look for an outlet or store to get things I needed. I purchased a dining room set, a bedroom set, and even a couple of pieces I had my eye on sometime back, but wouldn't get because of Gerald. I needed a sofa. The one at the house I had custom made and paid a pretty penny for it. I should get that one. I walked back to the living room furniture section and choose a sofa and 2 high-back chairs, a recliner for my bedroom, a beautiful octagon, glass, and marble coffee table with matching end tables and decided to call it quits before I went bankrupt in this place.

Walking to the cashier, I pulled out my talking memo minder and said into it, "Gerald, Be gone."

I pushed the button to play and the message played back. I started to laugh and felt like the weight of the world had been lifted from my shoulders. I knew the fight wasn't over but I would do whatever it took to survive this part of my life.

I paid with my MasterCard. The bill came to almost $7000.00. Luckily I had a $20,000.00 credit limit. It was worth every penny, knowing I didn't have to deal with Gerald. I refused to look back. I paid the store extra to have the furniture delivered that afternoon.

I went to Nordstrom's rack over in the East Bay and bought all kinds of household items. Kitchen towels, bath towels, little knickknacks. That was fun. Not fun on my credit cards, but fun. I felt like a kid with a new toy. This new freedom was like a high, not drug induced and out of control but natural and calming.

I got back to the house and started to unload all my new cargo. I remembered I had lots of things to still get from the house. I took only what I could pack-up at the time. This was what I hated about splitting up, all this starting over. The moving wasn't so bad, but I knew Gerald wouldn't make it any easier for me.

I sat on the floor and called the office. There was a message from Chantal. My secretary transferred me to her office.

"Nicole, how are you."

"Fine, Chantal, I've moved away from Gerald."

"Good for you. You have a lot of potential and I'd like to see you go all the way up the ladder."

"Thanks, Chantal, I've got the computer and everything set-up here, so I'm back on line, the fax machine will be working tomorrow." I'm going to be at home the rest of the week trying to settle in so I can be reached here."

"Nicole, its important you and Gregory get together in a day or so to plan what strategy you'll use in court on this case."

"I understand, please have the paperwork delivered so I can get started."

"I'll do that right away. You can expect them this afternoon."

"Thanks, Chantal."

"Bye-bye, Nicole."

Gregory was the attorney on the civil rights case I was working on. He was good but he didn't know the research software like I did. He liked to go before a jury and strut around like a Black version of Perry Mason. I admit he was so well dressed it made you notice him.

A lot of the female court employees took bets on how he would be dressed at any given time in court. This man knew his stuff; he was very good at what he did. He was so cool in the courtroom; you couldn't help but admire and respect him.

Chantal asked me to do the research to make sure it would be done to the fullest potential. Gregory was real full of himself. He thought he was all that and some. He missed his calling. He should've been an actor. Acting and lawyering all go hand in hand. He was good at both. He could do anything on cue, and his timing was always perfect like he had rehearsed for the role.

A great part of it was acting, and he knew civil rights law like he knew the clothes he wore. He had asked me, on numerous occasions, to go out with him and I refused. Well, those days were soon to be over, I was starting to feel better and better about being single again.

I called my mother to let her know I'd moved and how to reach me. We talked for a long time about her suspecting Gerald might be fighting me but she was glad I got away from him.

I called Sheila to tell her I got everything together. She wasn't at home, which I expected. I could call her cell phone number, but it wasn't important enough for that. I'd just leave a message on her voice mail.

I walked to the living room and looked out the window and saw the furniture truck backing into the driveway. They were on the ball with their delivery. I was just there less than 3 hours ago. I walked to the front door to let them in and get things set-up.

I started to try and make some organization out of the chaos in my place. I was really tired from all the day's activity. I put my feet up in my own house and felt wonderful. I remembered I had no food, not even a bottle of water in this place. Thank goodness the local grocery store would deliver because I didn't have the strength to go out. I made a list and called to have the things delivered to the house.

I fell asleep in the chair and awakened to the sound of the doorbell ringing. I looked through the peephole in the door to see who it was. It was the groceries. I paid the guy and started to put everything away in the cupboards. Looking in the cupboards, I was reminded I had no dishes, pots or pans. I refused to buy all that stuff all over again. I ate the leftover food from last night's meal.

I began to feel lonesome. I decided to call Gregory and get started with the case. He answered on the first ring.

"Hello, Gregory, this is Nicole Adams."

"Well Nicole, how nice to hear from you. When can we start to work?"

"Just as soon as I get the paperwork and familiarize myself with the case."

"I look forward to working with you on this. Chantal told me she made arrangements to have the papers delivered to your house." Gregory said.

The doorbell rang.

"Hold on please." I put the down the phone and answered the door. It was a messenger with the papers. He handed them to me and I signed a sheet. I handed him 5-dollars. He thanked me and left. I went back to the phone and apologized for the interruption.

"It's OK, Gregory said. I'm glad you have the papers in hand. I'll talk to you tomorrow at the office bright and early."

"No, I'm off the rest of the week to take care of some personal business." I told him.

"Oh, I didn't know."

"You can come to my house, so we can get started on the case in a day or two."

"Won't your husband be upset about that?"

"No not at all." I smiled to myself.

"Let me give you my new address and we can work on the case tomorrow."

"Sounds good to me." said Gregory and I could hear the smile in his voice.

I took the papers to the sofa and began to go through them. Gregory should be able to win this case with no problem. I thought.

He was a womanizer, but he was a good lawyer. It was rumored he and Chantal had a serious relationship sometime back, but neither has confirmed or denied it. So we didn't know for sure.

All the men at the office knew how jealous Gerald could be. No wonder Gregory said that to me. It was an embarrassment for me since all the men at my office knew Gerald was so insecure regarding my job.

I was whipped. I went in my bedroom and made up my brand new bed, with brand new sheets and took a shower and dried off with brand new towels and slept like a brand new baby.

Gregory called and wanted to get together later in the day to work on the case. I agreed and he was to come over around 4:00PM. I needed to call Gerald and make arrangements to get the kitchen stuff moved over to my place. I was not looking forward to this. I called the house, no answer. I called his job and he answered the phone. He never answered the phone at work.

"This is Nicole," I said.

"Hi Nicole, I miss you."

I ignored that and stated I'd like to get some things from the house.

"When," he said.

"Now would be good time for me."

"I'll meet you there in an hour."

The morning was getting off to a good start. No hassle with Gerald.

I didn't trust him, and I was somewhat leery of him, but I had to go there one last time.

I got up and got dressed. I put on an ethnic-flavored print tunic with matching pleat-front pants and a pair of black leather flats and was set to go.

I drove to my dream house for the last time and as I pulled up in the driveway I could see Gerald was already there. I put the key in the door and nothing happened. I tried again. I felt the door give, but because Gerald opened it. He stood there with this mocking smile on his face and I knew that jerk had the locks changed so my key didn't work. I refused to give him the satisfaction of that acknowledgment.

"Well Nicole, you been gone almost a week, you ready to come back home?"

"Get real Gerald. This is no game to continue to play with me."

I walked in the bedroom and saw Gerald had taken most of my things and put them in boxes. The closet was empty. The dresser still had all my cosmetics and such, in place. I got a box and put this stuff in it.

"Do you want me to help you, you deserter?"

"Look, I'm not going to stand here and let you insult me and call me names. Either you allow me to get this stuff out of here, alone, or I can call the police, and have them stand here while I finish what I need to do. The choice is yours."

"You know Nicole, I could kick your butt one last time for good measure."

"Yes, you could, Gerald. I could shoot you and put you out of your misery too."

"Take what you want! Don't come back here for nothing. All that you don't take this time around you can forget about it. Do you hear me?"

I heard the front door slam. I walked to the garage and looked out the window and saw Gerald getting in his car. That crazy fool! I thought. I'm glad he's gone.

I got busy packing everything I thought I wanted to take. I needed a small truck, but I'd just take what I needed and buy the rest. I'm taking the microwave, and the silverware, pots, pans, china. I don't pack carefully, I just pack. Anything that got broken, I'd throw away. I got the car loaded. The trunk was so full; I couldn't close it all the way. I found some string that was strong and tied it to hold the trunk down.

Finally, on my way to get this stuff unpacked and settled in. I planned a home cooked meal in my own place tonight. I got home and took the boxes into the house. I looked around and here I was again with my life in a bunch of boxes. Seemed like I was always moving. This time I was here to stay. I started in my bedroom. Hung up everything in the closet. Put everything on the dresser. This felt like my room, now that these things seemed familiar. The Linen closet was half full. I didn't take that much from the house, only what I thought was needed. I'd buy new linen. Linen that wouldn't have the smell of Gerald on them, or the old bloodstains that wouldn't come out through lots of washings, to remind me of times I wanted to forget.

Time to hit the kitchen. I would spend more time in here than any place else. I needed to make the kitchen feel nice and homey. This was where I did my best work. I got things in an orderly manner and walked into the living room. It looked like I'd been here for a while instead of just a few days.

I glanced at the clock and saw it was almost 4:00PM. Gregory was due any minute. I almost forgot he was coming. The doorbell rang. I answered and it was Gregory. I let him in.

"Hello Gregory"

I'd forgotten how good-looking he was. He looked like a Black Adonis, but I knew he chased every woman he could. I would maintain a professional relationship and nothing else with him.

"Hi Gregory, come in."

He came in and gave me a big hug.

"This is a nice place here, Nicole."

"Thanks, Gregory. I just moved in. I have a lot to do, but we have plenty of room to work on this case."

He handed me a bottle of wine. I took it and could feel the chill of the bottle through the bag.

"Would you like a glass of wine now, Gregory?"

"Sure, why not." he said.

I walked into the kitchen to get a glass and he followed me. I poured while he stood there looking at me with this smile on his face.

"Nicole, I assume you and that jealous husband of yours must be split-up."

"That is correct." I replied.

"I couldn't imagine being invited to your house with him there. I know he was crazy jealous about you."

"Listen, Gregory, Gerald and I are separated and will be getting a divorce soon."

"That dude was sick with it. I'm surprised he let you go without more of a fight."

Gregory didn't know the half of it, but it was no use airing all that dirt. So I just let it be.

"Come sit in the living room so we can talk more."

As I turned to walk back towards the living room, Gregory reached and pulled me into his arms. He kissed me on the lips and I backed away from him.

"What was that?"

"I always wanted to do that to you. You tasted like I imagined you would."

"I'm flattered and all that, but that's not the reason for you being here. If I'd just met you and we didn't work in the same company, I might be tempted, but I know you and I can't do it."

He looked at me and gave me that million-dollar smile and kissed me on the cheek, and said.

"Let's work on the case."

We worked until 1:00AM. I decided I had enough work for one evening, and Gregory stated he had an early morning appointment.

"I'll call you in a couple of days before we leave. Would you like me to pick you up for the airport next week?"

"That would be great." I said.

"Nicole, I want you to know I have a lot of respect for you. I know right now you're probably hurting, but you didn't once bring up any personal problem you might be having. I wanted you to know that. If you needed to talk to somebody, feel free to call me anytime. I'd like to continue being your friend."

"Thank you Gregory, I appreciate knowing you're there." I hugged him, and he said goodnight and left.

This was the part I hated. I forgot to make up the bed. They delivered it and set it up, and it's still unmade. I hate sleeping alone and being alone. I've been married 9 years and didn't have this to worry about. I knew Gerald would be home sooner or later, drunk or sober. I finally got the bed made and poured another glass of wine.

I thought about what Gregory said and how it felt to be in his arms. What was wrong with me? Was I so emotionally starved that it felt good to be in any man's arms? Could be. I sipped my glass of wine while standing in the doorway of my bedroom. I finally got the bed made and decided to take a hot shower and get some sleep. I finished the shower and crawled into the empty, cold bed. I lay there, and all kinds of thoughts started going through my mind.

I woke up to the sound of water running and realized the sound was coming from outside my bedroom window. I looked out and saw the sprinkler system was watering the lawn. I didn't have a clue as to how to set the system but it wasn't brain surgery so I would figure it out later.

I stretched and sat on the side of the bed and felt really good for a change. I had to find the paperwork for the system and see how to work it. Last night wasn't so bad after all. I looked around and noticed no pictures on the walls. I made a mental note to get my artwork from Gerald. What a jerk!

I got the cordless phone and brought it in the bedroom to call my office and check my voicemail for messages. I checked my voicemail box first. Four messages from Gerald and two from Montel.

I called Gerald first. I tried the home number and he answered on the second ring.

"This is Nicole."

"You finally decided to call back, huh."

"Yeah, that's right. We need to talk Gerald."

"About what, you took everything when you came the other day. "

"No, I didn't. You got all the furniture. The major stuff is still there."

"And that's where it will stay."

"Gerald you are a certified jerk"

I hung up the phone. I could see I was off to a great start this morning. I called my office.

Jason answered.

"Jason this is Nicole. Any messages for me?"

"Yes, you had some in your voice mail box. Would you like me to retrieve them?"

"No, I've taken care of them. Thanks."

"Nicole, we are busy here with this case and all, but with you working at home, you know what's going on.

By the way, I have the plane tickets for you and Mr. Taylor, and all the arrangements for your trip next week have been made. Should I have the tickets sent by messenger, or will you be picking them up?"

"Thanks, Jason, either me or Mr. Taylor will get them by the end of the week."

After a few more minutes of updates from Jason I was done.

"See you later Jason, bye, bye."

"Bye Nicole."

I remembered there was so much personal business to take care regarding my martial status. Car insurance, quick claim deeds to clear myself of financial responsibility with the properties Gerald and I owned. I had an advantage over Gerald with this legal stuff because I didn't need a lawyer, I could do all of it myself. How do you like me now Gerald?

I found my typewriter and typed all the necessary forms. I got them ready to be filed in court and served on Gerald.

I decided to take a break from all this madness and got dressed. No wonder people just stayed together and put up with the crap.

I put on a royal blue sleeveless tunic with a Kente cloth shoulder yoke and Kente trim at the waist and wrap style Kente crown for my head. I called my hairdresser and made an appointment for later in the day to get my hair done and a much-needed stint at the spa. I couldn't wait to get a massage and mud bath.

I drove to the post office to get a change of address packet for my mail. On the way back I stopped at Circuit City and bought a new stereo CD system. I bought some new CD's too. Now I could go back home and have some new music in the place.

Something told me to drive by my old house to check the mailbox for my mail. I did. As I turned the corner, Gerald was backing out of the driveway. He saw me and got out of his car and walked over to mine.

"Hey Nicole."

"Hello, Gerald."

"Nicole, what don't you come in the house so we can talk."

"No way Gerald, I don't trust you. Let's talk here. We need to decide how we're going to do the house. You can buy me out and continue to live there, or we can sell it. We've got the cabin in Tahoe, and the resort property too."

"Nicole, why can't you get over this and we save ourselves all this trouble. I started going to AA meetings again and I haven't had a drink."

"Look Gerald, we can talk about it now or later. It really doesn't matter. We need to resolve these matters between us instead of getting lawyers involved, and you know it."

"Yeah Nicole, I'll leave a message on your voice mail, since I don't know where you moved at.

I'll let you know next week on what I decide to do."

"Fine Gerald, I've got to go."

I drove away from Gerald and the house and I knew this would be the last time I had to deal with this. I'd never seen Gerald look so defeated. He had this look in his eyes, like he wanted some peace and calm as I did. I believed we would be able to settle this like adults, and not animals.

I hit the freeway and cruised on home. I put my car in the garage and took my new CD player and CD's into the house. I hooked it up, poured me a glass of ginger ale and thanked my God for another day.

Just as I was kicked-back, the phone rang. I snatched it up and said hello.

"Hey girlfriend," it was Sheila.

"Hi there."

"I'm on the way to your house and wanted to make sure you were there before I stopped by."

"I'm here," I said.

"I'll be there in 20 minutes."

Forty-five minutes later, the doorbell rang. I knew it was Sheila. Her time frame was later than everybody else's. Always had been and always would be. I opened the door for her as she strutted in.

"How was your first night here? Dang, girl you been real busy. Where did all this stuff come from?"

"Which do you want me to answer first?"

"The last question. Where did all this stuff come from?"

"I bought it."

"You didn't waste no time at all. Go on girl, this place is laid"

"I tried talking to Gerald to share some of the furniture and he wanted to hassle. I did the next best thing and bought my own."

"I heard that. I see you are just fine. It looks like you been here for months. You got your office all fixed up like you been working."

"I have. Gregory Taylor came over last night and we worked on a case."

"I'll bet you worked on a case. Said Sheila. "Yours.""

"That man was hand-made by God. I'd let him work on my case anytime he so desired."

I laughed at Sheila. She had a great sense of humor and you never knew what she might say cause she wasn't wired right.

"I'm out of here. Must take my laptop back to the dealer. It is not programmed right."

"I have a hair appointment in a while, call me later." I said to Sheila.

"OK."

I arrived home and wondered what to have for dinner. Boxes were still in the kitchen that needed to be put away. I started to unpack some more stuff. Today was Thursday, so I had the rest of the weekend to get everything in order before leaving for Los Angeles.

On Sunday night I called Gregory to find out what time he would pick me up. There was no answer at his home. I called my office to check the voice mail. The message was: Gregory had the tickets and would call me on Sunday night to confirm time of pickup.

I went into the bedroom to pack. Usually, I had myself together by now for one of these trips but due to the past week, I was behind schedule. I really resented Gerald causing all this stuff and causing me to have all these unnecessary changes to go through. I sat down on the bed and reflected on all that had happened just the past week. I looked around at this house and wondered. What in the world is going to happen to me? How many more bad decisions am I going to make? What is wrong with all these men I keep getting caught up with?

I pulled out the garment bag and started to pack. To travel in, I'd wear a black print jacket and matching vest, black slim skirt. For court, since that was still so conservative, I wanted to be stylish but yet professional, I'd take a silk, black floral long vest, and matching skirt. A button front, long sleeved white blouse. The skirt buttoned all the way down the front, and a pair of black leather pumps. That would work.

The phone rang. It was Gregory.

"Hi Nicole."

"Hi Gregory."

"I'm calling to let you know I'll pick you up at 7:00AM."

"That's fine. I'll be ready."

"I have all the tickets and hotel reservations with me."

"OK, I'll see you in the morning."

"Bye" Gregory said.

I continued packing. I found my briefcase and put in the papers, Gregory and I had been working on, and the laptop computer. I also grabbed a couple of DVD's just in case I had time to watch a movie.

I went in the kitchen to make something to eat. Couldn't find anything good, so I opened a can of soup. I only ate these days because it was necessary. The food had no taste and I had no appetite.

I should call Gerald and let him know I would be out of town on business. I called the house and he wasn't at home, so I left a message on the answering machine. That jerk, bet he wasted no time in getting with somebody.

I turned the TV on to watch, but my mind wouldn't let me concentrate. I kept thinking about what the future held for me, and it was scary to think I'd have to face it alone. I fell asleep in the chair. When I woke up it was 1:00Am. I moved from the chair to my cold bed. It was cold but it felt safe. I turned the alarm on for 5:30AM; otherwise I would never be ready when Gregory came. I slept like I was in a coma.

I woke up to the sound of Luther Van dross, crying about some lost love, and turned off the radio. Sorry Luther, but I couldn't listen to that sad song right now.

I got up, showered and started to get dressed, combed my hair, and put on a little makeup. After all of that, considering what I'd been through, I felt pretty good.

I wondered if Montel was at work. I picked up the phone and pushed the numbers.

"Computer room, this is Montel."

"Hi Montel, this is Nicole."

"Sweetheart, where have you been?"

"Listen Montel, I left Gerald a few days ago and moved into my own place on the other side of town."

I didn't want to bother you with my problems. That's why I didn't tell you the other day when we talked."

"Baby, you really left your husband?"

"Yes, I did. I got tired of him putting me in the hospital."

"He beat you down?"

"Yes, he slapped me around."

"Why didn't you tell me, Nicole?"

"I couldn't tell you. I was embarrassed and it's not something you tell other people."

"Nicole, when can I see you? I can leave work right now and come to you."

"No Montel, I'm getting ready to go on a business trip, out of town, and I called to let you know. This case has been all over the news, so watch your TV. I'll give you my address and phone number to my new home."

"You're going to be on TV Nicole?"

"Yep, I'm on the defense team for this case. I'll be doing all the research. I'll be sitting at the plaintiff's table with the lawyers."

"Wow, that is really something. You must be good."

"Well, I know my job. Have you heard of Gregory Taylor?"

"Yeah, he's the dude that won all that money for a Black family last year in a police brutality case."

"That's the one."

"You know him personally."

"Yes, for a number of years, we're friends."

"I had no idea, I was involved with a celebrity."

"I'm no celebrity. I just deal with high profile cases."

"I hear that brother loves the ladies."

"He does have that reputation."

"You'd better watch him."

"Come on Montel. Don't tell me you're jealous of him."

"No, not jealous. Envious. He's going to have you in a hotel, alone, vulnerable."

"This is business. Not romance."

"Business for you. If I were him, the temptation would be too much to put on any man, I assure you he will make a move."

" Montel, I've got to go. I have a plane to catch. I'll be staying at the Wilshire hotel."

"I'm sure calling sometime tonight. I'll talk to you then, sweetheart."

"Bye."

"Bye."

Just in case, I decided to take a pair of black slacks, black silk blouse and a tan, silk blazer. Tan shoes.

I picked up the garment bag, and it was heavy. I put the rest of my makeup in the makeup case and locked it. I was really proud of myself, only two pieces of luggage.

I took one last look in the mirror and I was glowing. My eyes were dancing. I didn't know what it was about Montel that made me feel so good. He made my entire being come alive. As I stood reminiscing about the conversation with Montel, the doorbell rang. I was pretty sure it was Gregory, but you never knew. One time before when I had left Gerald, he found me. He followed me from work. Someone knocked on the door and I just opened it without asking who it was. There stood Gerald in all his drunken splendor. I ended up calling the police to get rid of him but he wouldn't leave me alone after he found out where I lived. I ended up going back to him.

I looked through the peephole, and the voice said it was Gregory. I let him in.

"Good morning, Nicole."

"Good morning, Gregory."

"You look so pretty this morning lady. There's a glow about you. What did you do to yourself?"

"Nothing, I just talked to a friend this morning on the phone."

"That must've been some conversation is all I can say". "You are lit up like the 4th of July." We both laughed.

"You want some coffee or something before we leave? I asked.

"No thanks, would you mind if we left early so I could have a big breakfast? I don't like to fly and if I fly on an empty stomach, I'll get sick.

I did a last minute check of my house and picked up the two pieces of luggage.

"Let me take those for you." He took them and looked at me baffled.

"This thing is heavy." "Who do you have in it?" We both laughed all the way to the car.

Gregory and I arrived at the airport almost 2 hours before the flight was scheduled to leave. Neither of us bothered to check the baggage, so we went into a coffee shop to have breakfast. I wasn't hungry, but I had a cup of coffee and a sweet roll. Gregory had a huge breakfast and enjoyed every mouthful. Watching him eat was a work of art. I'm surprised he was in such good shape after watching him eat.

Finally, it was time for the plane to leave and they called us to board. We found our seats. The company paid for 1st class seating so there was more legroom. Gregory sat on the aisle seat and we started to go over our work. I pulled out the laptop and checked to make sure we were on line. I could access my office to keep them updated so I sent Jason an E-mail to let him know we were in flight. Jason E-mailed back to acknowledge. I put the computer back in my briefcase, and we began to discuss the case.

I listened to Gregory on how he intended to proceed, what he was trying to show the jury and the general strategy he planned to use to prove his case.

Before we knew it, we arrived at Los Angeles International Airport. We put all the papers away and started to exit the plane. We gathered our luggage and headed for the rent-a-car place. We handed the woman behind the counter the reservation and found the firm had rented this brand new sport turbo coupe something or another. This car was too tight. We both laughed like two kids with a new toy and both of us wanted to drive it.

I said, "Let me drive."

He said, "No, I want to drive."

We laughed all the way to the hotel. We checked into the hotel and went to our designated rooms on the same floor. His room was at one end, mine on the opposite end.

The time was only 10:00AM. We decided to unpack and head to the law library. I walked into my room, and it was really nice. A king size bed, a large, elegant bathroom and closet space you wouldn't believe. I proceeded to unpack. For the last few days, that's all I did was unpack. I laughed to myself. I put my slippers under the dresser and bathrobe in the bathroom.

I picked up my briefcase and purse and decided to call Gregory and make sure he was ready. The line was busy. I sat on the side of the bed and turned on the TV. My phone rang.

Gregory, said he just spoke with the client and informed him we were in town and needed to meet before tomorrow's court date we agreed to meet later that evening at the hotel.

"Let's get to the library so you can do your thing, and we can make sure we have our act together to win this thing." Gregory stated.

I noticed Gregory was all business, no joking.

He was tall and lean. He played tennis and golf almost every day. He was as black as the ace of spades but had the skin of a baby, smooth and flawless. He was immaculate in dress and had the social graces of royalty. He had eyes that appeared to penetrate your soul. They were a dark brown with a twist. They almost seemed to change colors depending own his mood and the situation he was in at the time.

We met in the lobby and headed for the library. We both had been here on numerous occasions, so we knew the area pretty well. I decided after the meeting was over, I'd go shopping.

We arrived at the library and worked until 3:00PM. Watching Gregory work was like watching a magician. He could do magic right before one's eyes. He decided we had everything we needed to go to court. I dropped him at the hotel, and we agreed to meet in the hotel restaurant for dinner and meet the client at 7:00PM.

I headed for the mall. I had on high-heeled shoes, so I wouldn't be doing a whole lot of walking. When I arrived at the mall, there was nothing I wanted. I decided to go in the yogurt shop and enjoy the different scenery in Southern California. The weather was smoggy. No wonder people had smog alerts. I finished the yogurt and headed back to the car. The time was 5:00, and the traffic downtown was a nightmare. I should have left a long time ago. Luckily, the hotel was only a few miles from here.

I got to the hotel and the doorman opened the car door and parked the car for me. He said the key would be at the desk. I thanked and tipped him.

I walked to the elevator and met this guy waiting for the elevator,

He said, "Hello."

I said, "Hello."

He asked if I was staying at the hotel.

I said. "Yes, I was."

He mentioned after dinner in the lounge there was jazz music if I was interested. I told him thanks for the information. I just might check it out. We got on the elevator together, and he got off on the 7th floor.

I went on to the 12th floor and got off.

I walked down to Gregory's room and saw the "Do not disturb" sign on the door. Did he meet somebody? I wondered. Oh well, if he did, lucky him. I felt a tinge of jealously.

I took off my clothes, put my bathrobe on, and lay down on the bed. It felt so good to relax and have on comfortable clothes.

The telephone rang. I reached for it thinking it was Gregory.

"Yes."

"Hi baby, its Montel".

"Hi."

"Did I get you at a bad time?"

"No, not at all, I just got back a few minutes ago." I said.

"Look Sweetheart, I can't get you off my mind. I've been thinking about you all day. When are you coming back?"

"In a few days maybe, I don't know for sure. It depends on how long this trial will take."

"Nicole, Baby, there is so much I want to say."

"I know Montel. I have a lot to talk to you about too. There are so many things I have to work out, so much to take care of."

"Baby, my life is not complete without you."

"Montel, you are a married man, still living with your family." I know you don't want a bigger mess than we already have."

"Don't worry about that Nicole. I'll handle it. Trust me."

"Montel, I have a meeting in less than an hour." I'll call you when I get home and we can talk some more."

"Nicole, you have a good night."

"You do the same, Montel."

I hung up.

The phone rang again.

Gregory said, "Yo, Nicole, you're back."

"Yeah, what's up?"

"Look, I met this lady, and were are going to hang out for a while. I needed to let you know, just in case I'm late for dinner."

"I'll cover for you. Angus Jackson will be fine with me."

"I have no doubts about that." Said Gregory.

"Should I make a reservation for your lady friend?"

"No, she's strictly a guest for tonight."

"You know, Gregory, you are a dog."

"Yes, I am. No, I don't turn down no freaks." Call me satisfied."

"Any excuse is better than none at all Gregory."

"Anyway, Nicole, she consented to stay, I'm not forcing her."

"Do your thing. I'm glad I didn't fall for your lines of crap."

"Nicole, I'd dump her in a heartbeat if I thought, I had a chance with you".

"Gregory, I'll see you eventually, at dinner. Goodbye." I hung up.

I got up to shower and dressed for dinner to meet the client. I never met him, but we had his picture on file, so I knew what he looked like. I got dressed and headed for the restaurant.

I saw Angus Jackson sitting at the bar. I went over and introduced myself to him, and he asked if I'd like a drink. I agreed to a ginger ale, and we started to talk about his case. I explained that Gregory had been detained and would be along shortly. I explained to Angus what to expect on the witness stand tomorrow and he seemed worried. I assured him Gregory was one of the best in the business. The client seemed reassured. He knew of Gregory's reputation.

Just as the conversation took on a lighter note, Gregory arrived all showered, shaved and ready to work.

"How nice to see you Mr. Jackson." Said Gregory. "I'm sure Nicole has filled you in on what will happen at the trial."

"Yes, indeed, she has. I'm ready to get this over and enjoy our dinner."

"I'm starved," said Gregory. He started to laugh.

I looked at him. He looked so smug and satisfied.

We went into the dining room and went over everything Angus needed to know and then ordered dinner and drinks. Everybody pretty much enjoyed the evening. Angus decided it was getting late and said goodnight. Gregory couldn't wait to get back to his free piece of tail for the night.

I remembered what that man told me earlier about the jazz music. Gregory couldn't wait to leave. As soon as Angus split, Gregory excused himself and almost ran to the elevator. He really was funny to watch when he was after a woman. He was the ultimate professional in the courtroom, but when it came to women, he fell apart at the sight of a pretty face. He was thirty something and had never been in a serious relationship that I knew of. He and Chantal was still a mystery, besides it was just a rumor they had dated once upon a time.

I headed for the lounge, and it was dark and smoky. The decor was pretty. I found a table up front and sat down. The waitress came over and took my order for a glass of Ginger ale. The guy I met at the elevator was at the microphone. He acknowledged my presence and started to sing. He was really good and so was the band.

After his set was finished he came over and asked if he could sit down at my table. I told him it was OK.

We talked about music and all kinds of stuff, and I found that we had lots of things in common, except he liked to get high, and I wasn't into drugs. He asked if he could order me another drink, but I declined the offer and excused myself. I left the lounge to go back to my room. I looked down the hall and tried to imagine what might be going on in Gregory's room.

As I entered my room, I thought of Montel. I undressed and got into bed. I left the light on in the bathroom, because this was a strange place, and I didn't feel secure. I couldn't fall asleep so I called room service and asked for a bottle of wine to be sent to my room. It took about twenty minutes. The delivery lady showed up and handed me the bottle. I handed her $10.00 and she left. I put the bottle down and I started to go over the papers one last time. I set my little alarm clock for 6:00AM. We were due in court at 9:00A.M. I fell asleep. I forgot about the wine.

I woke up refreshed. The phone rang.

Gregory said, "Good morning." I wondered did he have a good night?

"Good morning to you. You missed some good music in the lounge last night."

"Oh really! Nicole are you about ready?" He was all business now.

"Almost."

"We needed to get to the courthouse and check out the jury. I know who they were from the jury selection process. I want to see them, as they entered the courtroom to try and get a sense of how they would make their decision. "

"I can be ready in 1/2 hour."

"Good, I'll meet you in the lobby." He said.

I started to get dressed and the phone rang again. This time it was Chantal.

"Good morning, Nicole."

"Good morning." I said.

"I'm calling to wish you guys good luck today."

"Thanks, Chantal. We needed all the luck we could get. We've got a strong case, but you never knew how the jury would vote. Were up against the city of Los Angeles, and they were using their top guns on this one."

"Sometimes I wondered how I got in this case. "

"Believe me Nicole, if we didn't think you could handle it, no way would you be there. Everyone thinks you're a lawyer, anyway. Hurry up and go back to school, so you would be one, and it would be you down there today, trying that case, instead of Gregory, the womanizer." We both laughed. "Anyway, when you get back, I want you to come talk to me about the school thing."

"OK, you have a deal."

"Once again, to you and Gregory. Good luck. We know you will win, and we're depending on you. When you win this case, it will set precedence. It is a landmark case. Tell Gregory to do his thing for us."

"Will do Chantal." I said.

I took one last glance in the mirror and was pleased with the reflection. I looked professional, confident and good. I picked up my briefcase and headed out the door to meet Gregory. I found him in the coffee shop going over his agenda for the day.

"Hi," I said.

"Are you ready?"

"Yes," I replied.

"Let's go kick some City of Los Angeles butt."

They brought the car around, and we were off to the courtroom. When we got there, to avoid the media, we went around the back way, and there was Angus Jackson. We said hello and went straight to the courtroom.

The media was there and headed straight for Gregory. They asked if he had anything to say and he looked straight in the camera and said, no comment.

Cameras were allowed in the courtroom, so we all went to the plaintiff's table and sat down. There were cameras everywhere. I even saw one from court TV. I pulled out the computer and signed on to the office to keep them updated on the trial. I opened a file to keep track of any research Gregory might need for back up. I knew everyone at the office would be glued to the big screen TV we had in the conference room and, forwarding E-mails like crazy.

The jury arrived and Gregory kept a watchful eye on each of them. Everybody had arrived to get this show started. The bailiff called the court to order, and the defense team began their witness calling. Gregory sat and listened attentively, not doing much objecting. He was waiting for an opening. We had proof the defendants conspired against our client, but Gregory would wait until his time to cross-examine and present this evidence.

We listened to each witness and their testimony. You could tell they were professional witnesses but their testimony was weak. We knew it, and the jury had to know it. The judge called for a recess for the day. We would convene tomorrow morning at 9:00.

Some of Gregory's friends in the District Attorney's office offered to take us to lunch. I declined. Gregory accepted.

I drove back to the hotel and went to the room. It had been a long day, and I was hungry and tired. I got to my room and found a beautiful bouquet of red, long-stemmed roses. I read the card and it said: I miss you. See you soon. Montel.

My phone was blinking, I played back the message, and it was from Gerald. I phoned him back. He just wanted to know if things were all right with me.

"Yes." I said.

"Why didn't you tell me you would be out of town?"

"Gerald, I left a message on your machine." I could tell by his voice that he had been drinking.

"Nicole, I talked to a lawyer today, and he said you ain't gonna get nothing out of this house."

I knew where this conversation was going, so I hung up the phone. Gerald was drunk and nutted up on me once again. No lawyer had told him that. That house was bought with both our monies. Oh Gerald, please get a clue!

I went and read the card from Montel and smelled the roses. My appetite had come back for the moment, so I picked up the room service menu and ordered some dinner.

I undressed and put on something comfortable. I wanted to call Montel, but I refrained for now. The room service said it would take at least an hour, so I ran a tub of hot water and poured some milk bath under the running facet and watched the bubbles rise up in the tub. I poured myself a glass of wine and wondered what it would be like to make love to Montel.

I finally finished the bath, dressed in a lounge outfit and waited for the room service. There was a knock at the door and I looked through the peephole and saw it was my dinner. I tipped the guy, turned on the TV, and began to eat the dinner. My appetite was not getting better, so I had to force myself to eat.

There was another knock on the door, and it was Gregory.

"Hi," he said.

"Hi to you."

"I came to work on the strategy for tomorrow. I see you're having dinner, so maybe I should come back later."

"Why don't you in a couple of hours." I said.

In a couple of hours Gregory was back. I decided to put on a pair of slacks because, he kept giving me that hungry eye look and we needed no distractions in trying to win this case.

Gregory and Angus sat at the Plaintiff's table in the courtroom. It was Gregory's turn to call Angus to testify. Angus looked nervous but appeared confident. I sat right behind them with every reference book I thought Gregory would need. Papers, computer, and reference notes covered the table.

The courtroom was packed. The judge called the court to order. The bailiff called the first witness. Angus walked to the stand, was sworn in and took his seat. Gregory glided to the front of the courtroom, and all eyes were on him. He had on this suit that was tailored-made for him. The creases in his slacks were so sharp; they appeared to electrify the shine in his shoes. Everything about his presence echoed in the courtroom. There was no way he intended to lose this case, and that's the image he projected.

This was his moment, and he knew it. He went into his act. He spoke to Angus in a matter-of-fact tone of voice. His voice never changed octaves. He questioned Angus to the point of brutality, but his tone was so polite and gentlemanly one didn't notice the harshness. He completed the questioning and told the judge he was finished. Now he started to cross-examine the L.A. police department. He was matter-of-fact and polite. The one officer during his testimony took Gregory's politeness as weakness and that is when Gregory tripped him up so badly he started to stammer and stutter and couldn't get his lies straight. Gregory drove him like fast car. He left the witness stand a stammering mess. Gregory finished up with a summation that was beautiful. He looked at the defendant's table and gave them a smile that said, you loose.

The jury never took their eyes off him. He had to feel confident about that, for he had them in the palms of his beautiful hands.

As he glided back to the table, he winked at me, and I looked to the jury. They were smiling. I knew this case was soon to be over. The other lawyers laid the groundwork for Gregory and he stepped in and did what he was known for doing. Winning.

I could see he had planted the seed of doubt in the minds of the jurors. As he took his seat next to me, I congratulated him on a job well done. I E-mailed Chantal to let her know the jury had gone to deliberate. She E-mailed me back and told me to keep them up-to-date on the decision. Gregory and I headed to the nearest coffee shop to wait for the verdict. Angus chose to sit in the hall. We left him there.

Gregory told me, he could've done better. I told him he was magnificent up there, as well as brilliant. He gave me a smile that made me wonder what he would be like in bed. I totally understood why the women were at his beck and call. He was a real charmer. We waited seemed like for hours and nothing from the jury.

I wandered over to the window and saw all kinds of media outside. I would be glad when this was over, so I could go home. I had some direction on how to handle my life. I was so into my daydream, I didn't notice Gregory touching me on the shoulder. I turned towards him, and he told me the jury had made a decision. I felt a cold sweat come over me, but I gave Gregory a confident look, anyway. He had done a good job regardless of the decision.

We headed back to the courtroom, and the court was called to order. The forelady of the jury, handed the bailiff the paper, which would make or break or careers.

Gregory grabbed my hand and held it so tightly; I almost jumped out of my shoes. The judge read guilty for the City of Los Angeles. Guilty for police brutality, and guilty for civil rights violation.

Angus Jackson's financial problems were soon to be over. He had a long way to go dealing with the emotional trauma he had gone through at the hands of the Los Angeles Police Department. He had won enough money to pay for some heavy-duty counseling.

He had just won 5.8 million dollars, minus our 33 percent. I knew the city of Los Angeles would appeal but for now we were the winners.

Gregory released my hand and headed to the jury box where he shook each and every juror's hand. He came back over and had to practically pull Angus off of me, because he was so overwhelmed with emotion. He would be a celebrity. Every talk show on the circuit would invite him to come on their show. I hoped he wouldn't allow himself to be exploited too much.

We tried to make it out of the courtroom, but the media had to have an interview with the winning attorney and his team. I had a statement already written for Gregory to use for the media. I handed it to him, and he read it with all the charm of a hero. The video cameras were everywhere you looked. Finally the moment of truth was over and the media left to file their stories with their various newspapers and other print media.

Gregory and I were the last to leave the courtroom. We both stood there and enjoyed the moment. He walked over and gave me a big hug. He asked if I would like to go and have a drink.

I told him yes, but let's go back to the hotel, pack, and get a flight home. We could get a drink at the airport.

He said, OK, but I could tell there wasn't much interest in my idea. He looked so sad and unhappy.

"What's wrong?" I asked.

"Nothing. I was really hoping we could spend some time getting to know each other."

"Gregory, come on, we don't have that kind of attraction for each other. Sure, we could sleep together and unleash the curiosity. But I need more than that in my life. Can you live with that?"

"Yes, seriously, Nicole, this trial and the pressure are like a real turn-on. I'm sorry, Nicole. You are right. I have all these flings with women, but there's no one special to share these times with."

"Well Gregory, maybe feeling like this is a sign to tell you it's time to settle down with a special someone."

"If I slept with you, it would probably ruin a good friendship. I wouldn't want to do that, but girl I still want you." Gregory said.

"Gregory, you are too much." We headed back to the hotel.

I walked around the room and remembered I needed to call the office. I dialed the number, and Jason answered. "Hi, Nicole, we already heard." We had caller ID at the office so he knew from the number that it was me from the hotel.

"Angus Jackson called the firm a few minutes ago to congratulate you and Gregory on the case. Chantal and some of the bigwigs are in her office, planning this huge dinner gala in your honor."

"Nicole", Jason asked. "Just out of curiosity, how much money do you guys get?"

"I'll never tell, but you know when I get a bonus, my staff gets a bonus too. Without you guys being so good at what you do, we'd never be able to do what we do as well."

Jason laughed and asked if there was anything else.

I said, "No". "We are catching the next flight out of here." I hung up.

There was a knock at the door. It was Gregory and I was most uncomfortable letting him in. I needed to hurry and pack, so we could get out of here before I did something I might regret. I opened the door, and he was standing there all smiles.

"What is it," I asked.

"May I come in?"

"Yes." He came in and closed the door. He sat on the bed, instead of a chair. I ignored him and continued to pack.

"Nicole, It felt real good winning that case for Angus. I've been offered a job in L.A. in the district attorney office"

"Are you going to take it?" I asked.

I'm going to think about it very seriously. Maybe being here may help me settle down".

"Gregory, since you're sitting there, why don't you call the airport and make the reservation for home."

"OK, good idea."

He called, and we could get a flight out in 1 hour. finally, I finished packing, and we just talked. He came over and put his arms around me again. He held me so tight and it felt so good. I stepped away. I looked at him and he apologized.

"Let's go", I said.

I did a final check to make sure I hadn't left anything and we headed for the airport.

On the plane, Gregory and I talked about the case and the things surrounding the case and that was all. I could tell he was sad, because he had nothing of substance in his life. I could relate to what he felt, but I couldn't do anything about it.

Once in the air, the flight attendants were all over us, especially Gregory. It was his day to shine. We got all kinds of free drinks and champagne.

Finally the flight announced we were landing at San Francisco International Airport. Gregory and I left the plane, and the media was there, as well. Gregory talked to them, and I slipped away to find a ride back to the office.

As I walked down the corridor, I saw Jason, my secretary. He walked over to me, and gave me a hug, and stated he was there to give us a ride to the office. Gregory finally came over, and we were on our way.

We got to the office, and everybody gave us their congratulations. Chantal invited us in her office where the senior partners and junior partners had prepared champagne for us and catered a buffet luncheon. We enjoyed the moment.

Gregory come over to me and took my hand.

"You know Nicole, the verdict could've been the other way around."

I felt a chill in the air with that thought. It had been a perfect day. Everything was right. It was now time for me to go home and get my life in order. I made my exit from the office, and Chantal told me to take the next couple of days off. I thanked her and called a cab to take me home.

I arrived home and put my bags on the floor. I looked at the telephone and picked it up to call Montel. He answered on the first ring.

"Nicole, sweetheart, I'm so glad you're back. I saw you on TV and baby you were looking good. Can I come over?"

"Yes Montel, you can."

"I'll be there in about an hour."

I hung up the phone. My heart was beating so fast, I couldn't stand it. I was a nervous wreck. I picked up my bags and took them into the bedroom. I needed to call Gerald and Sheila. I dialed her number. She wasn't home. I left a message that I was back.

I started to unpack some of the things, but I couldn't keep my mind on what I was supposed to be doing. I don't know why I felt this way about this man. I just knew he made me feel so good. I continued to put away clothes from the trip. One of these days, I'll learn not to take so much stuff.

I decided to put on a CD that was romantic, and changed my mind. I didn't want Montel to think I was going to bed with him on the first day. I wanted to, but that would jack up my emotions too much.

The doorbell rang and I was so nervous, I had to stop and get a grip on my nerves. I asked who it was and the voice said, Montel. I walked over to the door and opened it. He came in and looked at me. I looked at him and he put his arms around me and hugged me. He kissed me on the cheek and then on the lips. As he was doing this, he pushed the door shut and continued to kiss me deeper and deeper. I couldn't see, hear or feel anything but what was going on at that moment.

His hands felt so good on my body. My body wanted to melt into his. His lips felt so good on mine. I stepped away from him to catch my breath. His hands never left my body. He had his hands on my lower back and he was caressing my shoulder and rubbing my back at the same time. It felt like he had more than two hands. They were everywhere at once.

He started to kiss me again, and I knew if I didn't stop him now, I never would. I felt him against me and knew we would soon be at the point of not stopping. I stepped back again, this time inviting him to sit down, so we could talk. He followed my lead and didn't take his hands or eyes off me.

"Nicole, there's so much to say to you. I don't know where to begin. I never thought I'd be in your house with you like this."

I know I hear you. I wanted to be with you, but it's not in my best interest to hook up with a married man."

"Nicole, I'm married in the legal sense. That's all. My wife and I haven't been together in a long time."

"Come on Montel, I've heard that before." Are you still sleeping together?" I asked.

Somebody rang the doorbell. I asked who it was. It was Gregory. Montel looked at me funny.

"Who was that?" he asked

"The lawyer at my office."

Gregory came in and I introduced the two of them to each other. I could feel the tension in the air. I didn't understand the tension, but it was there. Gregory stated he needed to get the notes I took from the case.

"I had them on the computer and would download on a disk for you." I said.

I didn't get this. He could've called for this information. He apologized for the intrusion and said he would call me later and left.

Montel commented that this man had more than just a passing interest in me. I said he didn't. Montel appeared to feel threatened.

"Come here. I want to hold, kiss, and make love to you the rest of this day."

He pulled me toward my bedroom. I was so tempted, but there was something stopping me. I told him no.

"Why not? You are separated from you husband, and about to get on with a new relationship."

"Wait a minute. I might be separated, but you aren't."

"So what?"

"You want me to move in here with you to prove my commitment to you, Nicole?"

"No, I don't Montel."

"Why not?"

"I think we're about to cross the line, Montel, and I want you to leave, right now".

"I think you're right Nicole that would be best. I thought we were going to have something. I'll see you later." Montel left.

I went to my bedroom and finished unpacking. I tried to sort out what just happened. Did Montel think I wanted him to move in here with me? Did he think I called him over to get in my bed? Am I wrong about him too?

The phone rang. It was Sheila.

"Hey girl, how you doing?"

"Fine", I said.

"How was the trip?"

Before I could answer, Sheila said she saw us on the news.

She said. "Girlfriend, you are a celebrity."

"No, not at all. Gregory is." I said.

"Girl, I see now, what you mean about him. He's a fine specimen of a man. He is all that and some."

"Look, do you have any plans for the evening?" I asked.

"No."

"Let's go out for dinner."

"OK."

"I'll pick you up at 8:00."

"Is that OK?"

"Sounds good, see you then." She hung up the phone.

I continued to unpack. I sat down on my bed and tried to figure out what just happened between Montel and me. The phone rang again. This time it was Montel.

"Before, you say anything, Nicole, I wanted to say, I came on too strong. I love you so much, I thought you wanted what I want."

"What did you just say Montel?"

"I said I love you so much."

"Do you realize what you just said?"

"Yes baby, I do. I lost it for a minute. I wanted to tell you this under different circumstances, but I don't want to lose you. When Gregory came over, I just checked him out and knew right away where that dude was coming from. I know you know too, Nicole."

"Come on Montel, Gregory is a co-worker and nothing happened between us." L.A. was business, you saw us on the TV. This was a big case."

"Did anything happen between you and him down there is all I want to know?"

"No, Montel." I'm still a married woman. That might not mean much to either of you, but it means a lot to me."

"I know it does, and I want you to take as much time as possible to do what you need to do, so we can be together. Look, baby, I need to go. Can I call you tomorrow?"

"Sure you can."

"Bye."

"Bye." Well all was right with the world once more.

I went in the bathroom to take a shower and get dressed for dinner with Sheila. We were going to Sugar's. Sheila was never on time. She said 8:00, but that could mean 7:30 or 8:30 or, whenever she decided to show up. It was now 7:13. I finally got unpacked, and most everything was put away. I needed to call Gerald, but I'd have to go through changes, so forget it.

Shiela arrived ahead of schedule. That woman never ceases to amaze me. She was dressed to kill or thrill, depended on who you were.

"Hey, What's up?" She asked. "You look like the trip did you good. Did Gregory give you his body? Is that why you look so happy? We both laughed.

"No, and only because I wouldn't let him. Montel came over today."

How could that be? Didn't you just get back a few hours ago? What did you do, call him from the plane? Did you Federal Express him a house key so he'd be here when you darkened the door?"

"No. Well, almost no. I called him, and he came right over."

"So did you sleep with him? How was it?"

"Sheila, shut-up for one minute." No, I didn't sleep with him. We sort of had a fight.

"Dang, Nicole. What's this, the second date? Novelty worn off already?" What was the fight about?"

"Nothing really, he wanted me to sleep with him, and I'm not ready for all that, plus he's still living with the wife."

"Nicole, Nicole, he's going to break your heart. That dude is no good. I haven't met him, but I know his kind. Please proceed with caution my friend."

"I intend too." I stated, knowing I had no control and had already crossed the line emotionally.

"Good thinking not to give it up so soon. Once they get it, the pursuit is over, and the relationship changes. They're no longer attentive to your needs."

"Oh, Sheila, you're so negative."

"Girl, you been married to Gerald too long. Things in the dating world have changed. These men are from another planet. Planet Stupid."

"Let's go have dinner." I said. We laughed as we walked to the car.

I got up from a restful night to the ringing of the telephone. I looked at the clock, and it said 6:00AM. I picked up the phone and before I can say anything, this sexy voice said. "Good morning."

I repeated the pleasantry and realized it was Gerald.

"What do you want?"

I knew I should've gotten an unlisted number.

"Nicole, why didn't you let me know you were back?"

I got defensive. "Why should I? I haven't forgotten the phone call at the hotel you made to me. Exactly what's up with that? Anyway, why are you calling me so early?"

What's the matter? Did I wake you and your boyfriend up?"

"Look Gerald, there's no one here but me."

"Tell me where you live Nicole."

"I don't think so. What I would like to do is get the rest of my things from the house and settle this matter between us."

"I saw you on the news the other day with that Gregory Taylor. Is he the one you left me for?

"Get real Gerald, you know who he is. You have always accused me of him or any of the other men at the office."

"Nicole, how much money did you make on this case?"

"Enough not to take crap from you ever again." I hung up the phone. It wasn't a good day. I called Montel.

"Hey lady." He said. "Let me take you to lunch. Better than that, this weekend coming up, let's go up to the wine country and stay at one of those bed and breakfast places. I promise you it'll be a week-end you won't ever forget."

I needed to think about that invitation.

"Don't say no, baby. Let me take you to lunch, give me your answer then. Be sweet. I'll meet you at Sugar's at 1:00. Be there." He hung up.

What am I doing? I knew this was leading to destruction. I couldn't stop it. All the warning signs were flashing and there was nothing I could do to prevent the approaching danger. My emotions had a mind of their own. I no longer had control. There was no logical pattern to follow anymore. Nothing mattered except being able to act and react on those feelings Montel caused me to have. Lord have mercy on me.

This house was starting to feel almost like home. I had everything into place finally, and I had a sense of being again. I still had those fears of self-doubt, but I suppose everyone does when it comes to not knowing what the next phase of life would be. I had a few more days to relax and unwind before I was due back at work. I wished I could talk to Gerald and get the process started but I knew that was only wishful thinking.

I really wanted to be with Montel, but I couldn't afford to get any more involved with him. I would call and cancel this lunch thing while I still had some control.

I punched Montel's number.

"Computer room, Montel Bradshaw."

"Hi, this is Nicole."

"Nicole, hey baby, what's up?"

"I'm calling because I have to cancel lunch. Something came up and I can't make it. We'll have to do it another time."

"Nicole, what is it with you? You say one thing and do another."

"That's not true at all, Montel." And anyway, why are you so demanding? We can do lunch anytime. At least, I can. I just called to let you know I can't make it."

"What are you doing this week-end Nicole?"

"I plan to finish taking care of some personal business. Why?"

"I'd like to be with you sometime this week-end."

"Call me, maybe we can get together."

"Well, Nicole, I've got to go. I have a service call, but can I call you tonight?"

"That would be fine, Montel."

"Later." He hung up the phone.

Montel was a computer programmer and worked some of the craziest hours.

I called Gerald. I had to keep trying to resolve this matter.

"What is it now Nicole?"

"We need to talk, Gerald."

"About what, Nicole? You chose to leave, as always. What is there to talk about?"

"I'm trying to be as civil about this as possible, but you just won't allow that."

"Look, Nicole. I won't bother you about jack anymore. I'm going to go on with my life with or without you. If you want to stay away, stay gone, but don't expect me to just put things on hold until you decide to come back. I have a woman, I want to be with, so don't come back here with a bunch of your crap and mess up my thing."

"Gerald, you can do whatever. Do what makes you happy. This'll be the last time I make any attempt to try and resolve matters between us. If you want to go to court and spend a lot of money, so be it." I hung up the phone. That jerk, I hated him. He could be with who ever he pleased as long as it wasn't me.

I knew this would come, and I'm surprised how I was handling it. I always thought when Gerald got with somebody else, I'd freak. I felt sorry for the cow really. Gerald had some problems no woman could resolve.

I spent most of the day changing all my business into my name only. I typed letters and memos to all concerned. Luckily, my car was registered to me only. I typed up some quitclaim deeds to all the property I didn't want and called a process server to serve papers to Gerald. He could have all of that expense.

"Here Gerald, give these to your new woman." I began typing up the divorce papers. This was one of the most depressing things I'd ever done. After having taken care of all of that, I felt pretty drained.

I make a sandwich and forced myself to eat half of it. I went into my bathroom and stepped on the scale. I had lost 8 pounds, not a good sign. I should call Montel back and apologize for breaking the date, but I needed to be alone and deal with these feelings.

The phone rang. It was Sheila.

"Hey girl." She said.

"Hi."

"How are you doing?"

"I'm fine. Hey, Sheila, let's go take a ride down to the coast."

"Sounds good to me. I needed to pack for the kids to visit their dad this weekend, but after that, I'm free as a bird. What time did you want to leave?"

"In a couple of hours is OK."

"You driving or me?"

"I'll drive. I just don't want to be alone right now."

"Are you sure you are all right, Nicole? Did you talk to Gerald today?"

"Yes, I did. I tried to talk to him about settling our private matters. He refused and told me he was about to get on with living and his new woman."

"That sorry piece of crap. Nicole, let the mother, live on. He was such a butthead."

I laughed. "Thanks, Sheila, I needed to laugh." I will pick you up in a while. See you. Bye."

"Bye."

I went into the bathroom and took a shower. I wanted to get dressed and get on the road. I felt much better. Some loose ends were finally coming together and I could proceed with my life. Montel, a married man. That was not my thing, but I was in love with him and I would have to deal with the repercussions. I prayed to God, the price wouldn't be too high.

What would I wear? On the coast, it would be chilly, so I thought long pants would work. I would wear my black rayon/wool, twill belted jacket, sleeveless clock print shirt and rayon/wool, hounds tooth pant. I'll need a low heel shoe for walking on the boardwalk so I decided on my black calfskin low heel pumps. I was good to go.

I arrived at Sheila's and she was ready. She came out and was dressed like a beautiful summer's day.

"Hey, where are you going with that backless, sleeveless, dress on? It's a beautiful dress, but we are going to the coast and you're going to freeze your butt off."

"I'd better get my coat." She said.

This girl must be in another time zone. I knew she saw the sun wasn't shining, and if she stayed home long enough to hear the weather report, she'd know rain was expected. I smiled to myself, as I waited for her to come back to the car. She was taking so long; I was beginning to wonder what she was doing. She finally came back out and had on slacks and a beautiful short, white leather trench coat.

"I liked that coat." I said.

We headed for the nearest gas station and hit the highway. As we got closer to the Monterey Bay Peninsula, it started to drizzle and pour down rain. We saw this Coffee Shop and decided to stop and have a cappuccino, and caffee macchiato. Sheila loved Caffee macchiato. I had to ask what that was.

The rain finally let up and we moved on. We arrived at the Monterey Fisherman's Wharf and set off to walk down the wharf area. It was really cold and windy. This was one of my bright ideas I shouldn't have acted on.

After walking around to all the shops in the wharf area, we decided to go and have a bite to eat. We chose a restaurant, and lo and behold who did I see? Gerald, and I guess, his new woman.

He saw me and almost broke his neck to come to the entryway where we were standing.

"Nicole, this is a surprise."

I bet it was I thought to myself. He looked like he wanted to break and run.

He started to stutter and stammer all over himself.

"Look, I don't care who you're with or what you do anymore. It's your life. Remember?"

I turned and walked out of the restaurant and met Sheila.

Sheila said, "That was a performance. Did you see that woman? She must've weighed in at 300 and counting. Is that what Gerald was so anxious to start his new life with? He's going to need to work harder at his business just to keep that big cow in food."

We laughed all the way back to the car and decided to stop on the way home for something to eat.

I dropped Sheila at her house and thanked her for going with me. She said, "I'll call you soon."

"Bye." I replied.

I arrived home and just dropped on the sofa. Today had been a day. It had been a turning point for me. Today I saw my husband, abusive as he might be, with another woman. I felt strange and awkward but I'm OK with it. "Dang Gerald your taste in women has changed.

I woke up to the sound of the phone ringing.

"Hello."

"Hi baby. It's Montel. Can I come over?"

OK, Montel, come on."

"I'll take you to dinner."

"I'm not hungry but you can come over."

I looked at the clock and realized it was almost 7:30PM. I had been asleep for almost 3 hours.

"All right, Montel, I'll see you in about an hour."

"Baby, I'll be there soon as I can. Bye"

I turned off the phone and got up to change clothes for Montel. I was excited beyond words. Tonight, I knew, he'd be in my bed. I could feel my body crave for him. I couldn't wait to be in his arms and let our bodies do all the talking.

I'd wear this royal blue fitted wrap jacket that ties on the side and matching skirt that has an asymmetrical front slit. I had a pair of satiny scalloped pumps that would go with this outfit perfectly.

After taking a quick shower, I got dressed and decided to have a glass of wine. I turned on the TV. It was one of those shopping channels, and they were featuring a phone and answering machine combo at a good price. I ran to the bedroom to get my credit card to order it. I placed the order and paid extra for two-day delivery. What a way to shop I said to myself.

The doorbell rang. I was sure it was Montel and I could hardly contain myself.

"Who is it?"

"It's me, baby."

I opened the door and let him in; I couldn't wait to be in his arms. He came inside the house gave me this smile that told me everything in it. He closed the door, and took me in his arms, and kissed me so deeply, I almost passed out from the fire that my body felt for him. He stopped kissing me long enough for me to catch my breath.

"Where would you like to go for dinner, sweetheart?"

At this point, who needed food, I thought. I suggested this place called Roses are Red. I could have a salad.

"Sounds good to me, "he said.

"Would you like some wine?"

"No thanks, I don't really drink wine. Do you have some cognac?"

"I sure do. How do you like it?"

"Straight up with no ice."

I went into the kitchen to get some ice and he followed me, as I reached for the ice in the freezer, Montel stood there watching. I could picture him standing there on a daily basis. There was so much I didn't know about this man. Perhaps I should have him checked out by an investigator I knew.

I walked back to the bar in the living room and Montel sat on one of the bar stools and I poured the cognac in a glass. He took a sip. I was standing next to him and he pulled me into his arms and began to kiss my face, neck, and I felt his hands begin to undo the top button of my jacket. I knew if I didn't stop him now, I never would.

"Montel, what time are we going to dinner?"

"Come on baby, who needs food right now?"

"I've been thinking about you all day. I broke all kinds of speed limits getting here, just so I could hold you in my arms." Montel said.

"I want to be in your arms, but there are some things we need to get straight first."

"Nicole, are you and Gerald going to get a divorce?"

The nerve of this man is unreal. Are you leaving your wife anytime soon? I thought.

"At this point Montel I don't see us getting back together this time." Things have gone too far to turn around. We have gone through this too many times in the past to keep repeating the same thing. We hurt each other. I've had enough. I had started divorce proceedings."

I had typed the papers. They were still on the computer disk.

"Why do you ask?" I asked Montel.

"Just curious is all. I want you. I want us to be together."

I really wanted to ask about his situation. He didn't mention it, so I decided to wait until another time. I walked over to where he was sitting and put my arms around his neck. He pulled me to him, stood up and we started to kiss again. I decided we better leave the house before we went too far. He agreed, and we left for dinner.

We finished dinner and decided to take a drive. The night was clear, and cool. As Montel was driving, I was looking at him and his eyes were sparkling. He smiled at me, and reached for my hand. He held it for a moment and dropped it ever so lightly in my lap. He reached over and put his hand on the top of my leg where my skirt had ridden up. I could feel the heat from his hand surge through my entire body.

We got back to my house, and he asked if he could come in for one more drink. I knew that wasn't a good idea. Feeling this way about each other would take us to another level if I allowed him to come in. I knew emotionally, I had a lot of baggage to unload. My heart said yes but my mind screamed no. I followed my mind. I told Montel it was late and I had an early morning. He accepted that and stopped the car as we arrived at the house.

He said. Well, I'll walk you to the door, anyway."

We walked to the door, and he kissed me one last time. I didn't want to let him go, and my lips and body told him so.

"Why don't you let me come in so I can answer all the questions your body is asking?"

"I have an early day tomorrow, remember?"

"Sure, Nicole, whatever you say. I'll call you tomorrow."

He kissed me on the cheek and left. I could tell he had an attitude.

I stood at the door and watched him walk away. I wanted to call him back but went on into the house. I walked into my bedroom and wished he were there with me to hold me all night. I put those thoughts out of my mind and got undressed. As I prepared for bed, I reminisced about the evening. I loved Montel, but I knew Montel was dangerous in any sense of the word. I knew Montel was going to break my heart but I was willing to take that chance. I fell asleep thinking about Montel's lips on mine.

On Saturday, I woke up and found that I had gotten a good night's sleep.

The phone was ringing. I'd be so glad when I got my answering machine, then I wouldn't have to answer the phone.

"Good morning." I said.

I recognized Gerald's voice on the other end.

"What do you want?" I asked.

"I want you to come over and get whatever else you want from this house. I've decided to sell it, give you your share, and move someplace smaller."

"Why is that, Gerald?" I didn't trust him.

"Because, I gave some thought to what you said, and you were right about the lawyers fee and all that. I don't want to fight anymore with you. You were right to leave. I was wrong to hit you. I'm going to get professional help with the drinking and try to get my act together."

"Too bad you couldn't do it when we were together, Gerald. Maybe, this mess wouldn't have happened."

"Sure you're right Nicole, if I change, will you come back?"

"Gerald, we've been through this too many times. It's time for both of us to move on. We only hurt each other. Together, we make an unhealthy pair. I'll come by when I get some time. I'll call first."

"There is one thing I want you to know, Nicole. You will always be the only one I'll ever love. We've been to hell and back and you were there for me. I'll never forget that. I hope whoever you get with, they make you happy and treat you right."

He hung up.

Well, he sure had a change of heart all of a sudden. I wondered what happened. Maybe, he finally realized his problems and would do something about them.

I got out of bed and took a shower, made a pot of coffee and sat in the lounger to ponder the morning's event.

I called Gerald to see if he would be there so I could get my paintings. Those four paintings cost a fortune, and I was going to fight Gerald for them. He would be there for the next couple of hours.

I parked in the driveway and walked up to the door. Gerald saw me before I saw him. The living room was empty. I didn't ask any questions. I saw he had taken down the paintings I wanted and stacked them on the dining room table.

"I see you didn't waste any time hauling your butt over here." Gerald said.

My stomach began to knot up. I judged Gerald wrong. All that talk was a ploy to get me over here. Gerald looked like he had not slept all night, and I could smell the booze coming from him. As a matter of fact, he had almost an aura of haziness around him.

I didn't say anything. I gathered up the paintings and headed for the car. I left my purse on the counter in the kitchen. I had to go back. I walked back to the door and he stepped aside. I got my purse. I had more things there, but it wasn't worth the hassle. I said good-bye to Gerald and headed for my car one final time.

As I drove away, I saw Gerald standing in the door. I didn't feel sorry for him, because he made my life hell. I knew this time in my heart this chapter of my life was closed.

I stopped at Nelson's coffee house to get some breakfast and, surprisingly, I was hungry. I got coffee and leisurely enjoyed the moment. After finishing breakfast, I decided to head for the Rose Garden Park. This time of year the roses were beginning to bud.

I arrived back home and took my paintings out of the trunk and put them on the sofa until I decided where to hang them. The phone rang and, it was Chantal.

"We are having a dinner party in honor of you and Gregory, next Saturday. It will be semi-formal and we'll send a car for you, so you can drink as much champagne as you like. Your staff is invited as well."

"That sounds like fun. Thank you. Have you told Gregory yet?"

"I have been trying to call him for the last couple of days with no answer, so I left a message on his answering service. I have yet to hear from him, though. "

"Well, maybe, he's out of town or something."

"Could be," said Chantal. "Anyway, just so you know. Next week, I need you here at the office, so I hope you have all your personal affairs in order. I might as well tell you first that I will be leaving this firm in a month. I have taken a position with a county agency where I can do some good for the children."

I was stunned by what she had just said.

"Chantal, this is a surprise. Was this planned?"

"No, not really, Nicole. The opportunity just sort of presented itself, and I'm going to take advantage of it, as you should about going back to school. I'd like to see the arrangements being made for you before I leave. Anyway, next week we'll talk, OK?"

"OK."

"Goodbye, Nicole."

I heard the line break, so I hung up the phone and sat down. I was in tears. Chantal had been a good friend and mentor. She had been through so much over the last few years. I was going to miss her.

I thought. Everything is changing. I better get my act together. Chantal wants to help me get into a law school. I started making arrangements to get transcripts and making a list of the schools to which I'd like to apply.

I was so absorbed in what I was doing, I was startled by the sound of the doorbell ringing. I got up and asked who it was. It was the Federal Express man, I opened the door, and he handed me something to sign and than handed me a box. I realized it was my answering machine. This shopping by TV was great!

The workweek started and I was back after what seemed like days. It was busy. Jason brought in all the phone messages I needed to return to clients. Most of the day was spent on the telephone.

Chantal brought a project for me to work on. A project requiring legal research on a police brutality case in San Francisco coming to trial. Our firm would be handling it. It was shaping up to be explosive.

The celebration party was this coming weekend, and I didn't have a date, so I would go alone. Maybe, I would ask Sheila if she wanted to go. She could bring a guest if she liked. I hated the idea of being divorced. These functions always required a mate.

My position at this firm had a lot of social functions. Gerald, most of the time, was able to attend them with me, but those days were over.

As I sat at the computer terminal, Jason buzzed my office and said Mr. Taylor was on the line. I put him on the speakerphone and said hello.

"Hi, there Nicole, I know this party is coming up for us, so I was hoping I could be your escort for the evening."

"That'll be all right with me Gregory. I was wondering who to attend this thing with? Just remember, you're my escort, and that's all."

He laughed. "I don't have a problem with that. They're sending a limo for us, so I'll have the driver pick me up first and then you."

"OK, Gregory." I replied.

"I'll have some news to share with you, but I'll wait until the week-end."

"See you then."

"Gregory are you coming in the office this week?"

"I don't think so, Nicole. I'm working on a case in another county, so I've been doing much of the work from home. The case isn't that complex, so, if I need something, usually my secretary can accommodate the things for me. How are you adjusting to the single life?"

"I'm coming along."

"Well you take care, and I will talk to you soon." He hung up.

I went back to work. I was a little apprehensive about being escorted by Gregory. This was a social function for work, but Gregory had tried to hit on me before so I didn't trust him totally. I didn't think he'd try anything, but one could never be too careful.

I looked at my watch and realized the day was almost gone. I decided to take a break for lunch. I went to a restaurant that I frequented and had a salad with a million-calorie dressing to try and gain some of my weight back. I was too tall to look like a waif.

After an hour-and-a-half lunch I headed back to the office and found a message from Montel on the desk.

I punched his number, and he answered on the first ring.

"Hello, Bradshaw."

I heard his voice, and I was dumbfounded. I paused for a moment and took a deep breath.

"Hi," I finally said back to him.

"How is everything?"

"Pretty good."

"Nicole, I've been thinking about you and me a lot. I wanted things to be right between us. I realize you're getting out of a marriage, and I'm still in one. Believe me, it's only a temporary situation with me. I've been planning to leave for a long time, way before I met you. My wife and I have been separated various times. We have a marriage of convenience. You know, I've never told you this before, but when I married my wife, I married her, because she was pregnant. That was the right thing to do at that time."

I listened to him, not only was he good looking, he had values. Little did I know his values only benefited him.

Montel went on. "I was engaged to someone else, and my wife, whose name is Benita, informed me of her condition. The other woman was devastated. She went back to her hometown to get on with her life, and I've held that against my wife. Over the years, Benita and I tried to make a go of it, but it has never worked."

"Montel," I interrupted. Have you kept in contact with this woman over the years?"

"Yes, I have. It's over, but we talk from time to time."

"Well, Montel, sounds like you have some things to work out, but I need to go finish my work." Maybe, we can talk some other time."

"Nicole, can I come over?"

"Not tonight."

I realized I couldn't put him off forever, but I could put him off for now.

"Nicole, we're adults here."

"I'm aware of that, Montel."

"So, what is the problem?"

"There is no problem."

"Nicole, I don't understand you with this crap, but I can only go along with your program right now. I'll talk to you later." He hung up the phone.

I turned the speakerphone off and stared into space. Had I lost him by playing hard to get?

Jason came into my office and handed me more work. It Looked like I would be here until late in the evening.

I arrived home, and it was almost 10:00P.M. I was wiped out. I checked my service for messages and found all beeps and no message. I worried for a moment and suspected it was probably Gerald. He would do some stupid stuff like that. I could've star 69ed it, but it wasn't that important right now. I was too tired. I found a message from Montel, but I would call him at a later date. I took a quick shower, had a cup of soup, and went to bed. I slept the sleep of the tired and worn out.

Today was the last day of the workweek. I still hadn't shopped for anything to wear to tomorrow night's gala event. It was being held at a restaurant near the San Francisco Airport.

I finished my work and called it a week. I told Jason and the rest of the staff, I'd see them tomorrow night and take off early. This job was important, but so was spending time with family and friends.

I headed for this dress shop I frequented and found this wild rose vintage look in a multi-slit dress with open back and retro jacket in beige. I had some beige pumps already, so I was good to go.

I stopped at this lounge on the way home to have a glass of wine. Who did I run into but Montel.

"Hi," he said.

"Hello," I replied. "What are doing on this side of the world?"

"I brought a customer of mine here for a drink."

"What are you doing in here all alone?"

"I came for a glass of wine."

Curtis, the bartender, came over and took my drink order.

"You know Curtis?" Montel asked.

"Yes I do. I've known Curtis for years." Montel looked at me funny.

"Small world, huh?"

"Sure was." I said.

Montel sat down and we talked for a few minutes. He said he had to get back to work and would see me later. He kissed me and made his exit.

Curtis come over and asked about Gerald. I left the booth, sat at the bar, and told Curtis the whole sordid story about our separation. Curtis said he was sorry to hear that, but that was life.

"Some things can't be worked out. Nicole, I don't want to get in your business but I'm going to ask you anyway. Are you hooked up with Montel?"

"I know Montel, Curtis." We are friends."

"Do you know that dude is married?"

"Yes, Curtis, I do."

"Yo, Nicole, you're my girl." Just wanted to check. Be cool".

I finished my wine and left for home.

I arrived home and found all beeps on the answering machine. I refused to call Gerald. I believed it was him but I couldn't prove it. What other idiot would do this?

This had been a long hard week for me, but I survived. I looked forward to tomorrow night's affair. No Gerald to get drunk and act a fool. I could enjoy myself.

The phone rang, and it was Montel, explaining he couldn't come over tonight.

I didn't invite you over, anyway, I thought.

"Nicole, I'll see you tomorrow night."

"No Montel, I have plans."

"With who?"

"With my job". I answered.

I didn't like being questioned like this. This man was married and still living with his wife. What difference did it make to him, anyway?

"OK, I'll call you tomorrow." Montel said.

The line went dead

He hung up so abruptly when things didn't go his way.

I called Shiela, and she wasn't home. I changed clothes, plopped on the sofa and fell asleep watching the shopping channel.

The weekend was finally here. Tonight was the celebration for the office and Gregory. Gregory hadn't called to confirm with me of the time he'd pick me up. Just as I thought this, the phone rang. It was Gregory.

"Hi" I said to him. "I was just thinking about you. His voice got low and dreamy.

"What were you thinking, Nicole?"

"About what time you'd pick me up."

"It starts at 8:00, so say 6:45. If we hit traffic going into the city, forty-fives minutes should get us there in plenty of time.

"OK, I'll be ready."

"You know the firm has gone all out for this. We get bonuses, trips and all kinds of perks."

"I only get bonuses. Good ones. I'm not complaining." I said.

He laughed and said. "Well, when you get your degree, you'll get all the fringe benefits too."

"I hope to. I'll be going back to school as soon as I can arrange it. I know you heard Chantal is leaving."

"Yes, I did. I'm going to miss her. She's one great lady. Her talents are wasted here. She's making the right career move for herself. I'll stay in touch with her. I have a special place in my heart for her. I almost married her, you know."

"No, I didn't". I said surprised.

"I had known Chantal for years before she came to work at this firm. We were real tight. I proposed, and she refused. Its funny how things worked out. If she had married me things would have been so different for her."

"Well, Gregory, that explains how she knows you so well. I have talked with her on very personal matters, and she never once mentioned she dated you or really knew you that well."

"I know. She asked me to keep quiet about it. It was a long time ago, anyway. Nicole, I have to go now. See you tonight. I intend to enjoy tonight like it was my last night."

"OK, Gregory, bye."

That seemed like a strange thing for him to say. I wondered if he was leaving too. Strange things were going on here. I moped around the house until mid afternoon and decided to take a nap to be refreshed for tonight.

When I woke up, it was almost 6:15. Oh gee! Gregory would be here in just a while and I wasn't ready. I rushed to take a shower and get dressed. I took my new outfit from the closet and put it on. It fit like a glove. The color made me look serene. The phone rang.

"Hello."

"Hey, what's going on with you?" Sheila said.

"I'm getting ready to go out."

"Out with who girl?"

"Gregory."

"Girl, that fine man is all that. I thought you weren't interested in him."

"Shiela, this is the party for us winning that case, remember?"

"I'd go out with him even if you'd lost the case."

"I've got to go, he's picking me up in a little while and I'm not ready."

"Have a good time. I'll call you tomorrow and you can give me details on the evening. See ya."

Shiela was totally insane. She's staying in for the evening with one of her boytoys, however this one has been around for a while so maybe she's more serious about him than the rest.

Speaking of insanity, how could I oversleep on such an important event as tonight? It was almost time for Gregory to get here. I might make it. I finished my makeup, and the doorbell rang. I asked who it was, and it was the limo driver. I let him in. I picked up my bag and headed for the door to let him in. He escorted me to this shiny, black, Lincoln, ultra stretch limousine. This car was tight.

As I walked to the car, the neighbors said hello and stared at me and this White man, as he opened the car door for me. I entered the car, and there sat Gregory, looking like he had been carved from black granite. He looked as though he had been drawn by an artist, and every detail had been perfected and captured on canvas to last forever.

I sat down, and he complimented me on how nice I looked. I mentioned to him, how handsome he looked. He smiled that charming smile of his and proceeded to open a bottle of champagne. The driver took off and we were on our way.

Gregory took my hand as we made our entrance. As we entered, the people from the office applauded. I could tell Gregory hated all this attention, but he handled it gracefully. I enjoyed any attention I could get. It would all pass anyway and back to business as usual.

We danced, ate, drank champagne and had a good time. Everybody from the office was there decked out in all of their finery. We talked and laughed with everyone. That was one thing I liked about this office. No matter where you worked in the firm, you were treated with dignity and respect. The janitor to the senior partner all got together to participate in the victory. This firm's corporate instructions believed in teamwork and these parties showed the aftermath of what teamwork could produce. They also encouraged you to reach any goal you set for yourself. If they saw you wanted to climb up the ladder, they were there to encourage you and do whatever it took to get you there. No wonder they had such a family oriented business. There were several employees there, that had started at the bottom and were now in law school or had gone on to private practice but they never totally left the firm. You could depend on them to give whatever support they needed when asked.

Gregory and I danced. He held me tight on a slow song. I could feel his breath on the back of my neck. I was glad when the dance was over so I could get away from him. While we were dancing, he told me he decided to take a position in the same city Chantal was moving to.

Chantal came over and hugged me. Gregory excused himself. Chantal said that she and Gregory had been talking, and they might try to have a relationship again. I was stunned by all this news. I guessed Chantal knew what she was doing by getting back with Gregory. Who knew and besides that, who cared? I could see Gregory standing at the bar watching us. One of the other attorney's from the office came over to ask me to dance, so I let him lead me to the dance floor.

After the dance, I found a seat and some people came over from the office and started to converse about office gossip. I made an exit and decided I had had enough for one evening. I found the driver to take me home. I told everyone goodnight and left.

The time was 2:00 in the morning. When was the last time, I'd been out this late? I felt like I had been to a Ball. On the way home, I thought how two people like Chantal and Gregory might complement each other's lives. I smiled to myself. Those two had been carrying on all along. I didn't know who they were trying to fool. I'm glad I kept my relationship with Gregory strictly business.

I arrived home. The driver got out and opened the door for me. He walked me to the door and said goodnight. I was sure the company had paid the bill for the limo service and all, but I tipped this guy $25.00, anyway.

"He said, Thanks, Ms. Adams."

I went inside my house and closed the door. I took off my shoes and got half undressed when the buzzer rang.

I felt my hair stand up on the back my neck. Who could that be at this hour? I asked, who it was. The voice said Montel. I opened the door.

"Hi," he said. "I've been waiting for you for 2 hours." He doesn't give me time to answer before he started to smother me with kisses. Deep passionate kisses. He picked me up and took me to the bedroom. He slowly unzipped my dress. I wanted to stop him.

Between the champagne, the moment, and my emotions, there was no way to win this war.

Everything in me was screaming. This man had awakened nerves that had been asleep for a long time. I stopped him long enough to ask what he was doing here at this time of night. He looked at me and said he left his wife and wanted to be with me. I was elated at the same time as shocked.

"Where will you stay?"

'I'll find a place tomorrow. I wanted to spend this night with you. I can't take this pressure anymore, baby. I want you so bad."

He had taken my dress and bra off. He was so smooth; I hadn't realized they were off. His shirt was off, and I could see he lifted weights by his body build. He continued to kiss me, my face, my lips, my hair, everywhere. I gave in. I wanted him as much as he wanted me, and now he was here. That's all I needed to know.

We got into bed, and it felt like he had a thousand hands. He touched me with his tongue, fingers, and hands. He kissed me everywhere. Finally, the moment of truth had arrived.

He slipped inside me, and I felt the world around me start to move. I felt his body tense, relax, and tense again. We were all arms, legs, and one body trying to reach a common goal. I was kissing him everywhere. Face, hands, eyes, and muscles. The sounds and smells of lovemaking permeated my bedroom. My body felt like it was on fire, and I could feel him taking that fire to a level of destruction and frenzy.

There was no me, no him, only here and now. My body was a roar and a scream that only a thrashing, wild, out of control, passion filled lover could make up close and personal. I reached the point of no return and felt the fire cross the fire line and destroy everything in its path. I held on with all my might until the ride came to an end.

At that instant, I could feel both of us reach the ultimate climb to the top of physical satisfaction. We held each other ever so tightly and allowed that final burst of passion to subside. The moment was magic. There was silence in the room. There was nothing to say. It had all been said.

I woke up first the next morning and found Montel's arm around my waist. I didn't move, because I didn't want the moment to pass. I lay there thinking about last night and how powerful all that was. I stared at Montel, and he opened his eyes. He pulled me to him and kissed me deeply. I put my arms around him and held on to him for dear life. We lay like that for what seemed like hours, not talking but letting our minds and body communicate for us.

I got up to go to the bathroom to take a shower. When I came out of the shower, Montel was up in the kitchen making coffee. I had pictured him in this kitchen, and he looked like he belonged there.

"Good morning," he said. He walked over and gave me a kiss. "You smell good."

"Thanks."

"I made coffee if you want some. I needed to take a shower and get to work." Montel said.

He put his pants on and went to his car. I watched him walk to his car and couldn't help thinking about last night and what a time we had.

He came back with a leather case.

"Montel, Did you really leave your wife?"

"Yes, Nicole. I needed to find someplace to stay. I couldn't go on living there. My kids don't understand, they think I've deserted them. I'm going to try and maintain a relationship with them despite what Benita may tell them."

He went in the bathroom to shower and shave. I sat on the couch and tried to get a grip with what was going on. Montel finally finished and came out. He said he had most of his clothes in his car. He walked back out to the car a second time and brought some things in. I had a strange feeling. How dare this man assume he could stay here. He took the clothes into the bedroom and changed into them. I remained sitting on the sofa. Last night was all that and some but I wasn't so sure of this moving in with me.

"Nicole," he said. "I'll see you later. I'm going to look for an apartment."

"Well Montel, I guess you can stay here for now. I was watching you and thought it awful presumptuous on your part when you brought those clothes in here. I thought you meant to just stay here without my having anything to say."

"No, Nicole, I wouldn't do nothing like that. I need to go. I'll see you later."

He pulled me in his arms and hugged me real tight and gave me a kiss that made me want him to stay.

I went back into the bedroom and lay across the bed. I lay on the pillow; Montel slept on, and inhaled his scent. The phone rang to interrupt my thoughts.

"Hey," said Sheila.

"Hi," I said back.

"How was the party?"

"The party was a lot of fun. Chantal and Gregory are hooked up."

"Get out of here." Said Sheila.

"Yes, Gregory told me, and then Chantal confirmed it."

"What a dog that Gregory is." said Sheila. "He was on you hot as stink on crap and still smelling in behind Chantal."

"I'm glad I followed my mind and not my body on that one."

"I hear you girl."

"You'll never guess what I'm going to tell you next."

"What is it now?" Sheila asked with concern in her voice.

"Montel is moving in here with me."

"You've got to be jiving me." Said Sheila.

"No, he was waiting for me last night when I got home, and he spent the night. He informed me he has left his wife, getting a divorce and needs someplace to stay, so I invited him to stay."

"Well, Nicole, I hope he makes you happy. I think he moves too quickly to be trusted myself, but you know I don't trust any of them. They are so sneaky and untrustworthy in my book. I use them like they use me. I don't need any of them, except for their maleness."

I changed subjects to get Sheila off her soapbox. I understood her feeling to the max, but I didn't want to give up on all men.

"Nicole just be careful. Married men don't usually leave their wives. You know you are my girl and I want you to be happy"

"I know you are concerned not just hating on me."

"I will call you later"

"ok"

"Bye-Bye"

"Bye"

I got up, got dressed and decided to make Montel a dinner fit for a king for his first night here. I went to the store and enjoyed the shopping and the whole trip. This was the way it was supposed to be.

I loved him, and he loved me. That was why this dinner would be so good.

I arrived back at the house and started to make dinner. I cooked like there was no tomorrow. There was enough food to feed a lot of folks, like the whole block. I really got carried away.

I set the table like I did when Gerald and I were together. While cooking I decided to put on a CD and I started to sing along with the music. I heard the doorbell and realized it must be Montel. My heart started beating so fast, I had to stop and compose myself.

He came in kissed me, and told me how much he missed me.

He said, "What are you cooking? You can smell it down the block. It smells so good."

"I made dinner for you. I wanted your first meal here to be special."

"I see," he said. "Come here." He pulled me to the sofa and made love to me again. His lovemaking took me to a place I'd never been before and hoped I could return to again and again.

We sat down to dinner, and I ate like I hadn't eaten in a long time. We had a good time talking and laughing and eating. Finally we were done and I loaded the dishwasher, and Montel went to bring his things in the house. I asked him to put his things in the spare bedroom, because there was more closet space. I continued to clean up the kitchen and finally finished. I went into the bedroom, where Montel was and got undressed. I put on this clingy silk gown. I Noticed Montel had stopped doing what he was doing, and I had all his attention.

"You know, Nicole, Gerald was a lucky man."

Montel came over to the side of the bed and started to kiss me all over my body. He took the gown off, and we traveled to a place where only passion and emotion had a reservation.

Today was the start of a new workweek. The place was abuzz with the changes taking place. Gregory and Chantal leaving was the talk of the office. Chantal had me doing all this research. I couldn't get Montel off my mind. I could smell his scent on my skin. I had him in my bloodstream. He was like my lifeline. If I didn't have him, I couldn't imagine not being with him. It was like being addicted to a drug of some kind though I had never done drugs, and the only way to feed the addiction was to see, feel, and be with him.

Time was passing so fast. Montel and I had been living together for a few months and all was well with us. I couldn't have been happier.

Gerald called from time to time but only to complain about silly things. He had heard, I was living with somebody and usually called to threaten me about all I'd lose in the settlement because of my adulterous behavior. Most times, I just hung up on him or pacified him, anything to get him off my back. We finally agreed to split the money from the sale of the house. I told him to keep all the money, if that meant he'd leave me alone.

A lawyer friend of mine suggested that I was making a mistake, but Gerald agreed to give me half of the money, which I was entitled to, anyway.

My birthday was in a month. The holidays were here, and Montel wanted to introduce me to his children, Cherish and Rajani. I had met his parents and sisters. His mom was a nosey, meddling woman and I was glad she stayed home and did her best work from the telephone. Her phone line was always busy.

Montel's wife had the phone number, she insisted on calling all hours of the night and hanging up whenever I answered the phone. This was causing plenty of friction between Montel and I.

I loved Montel with all my heart, but he was starting to get on my nerves. He was a slob. He was also a chauvinist pig. He had been living here for a few months and had yet to contribute to anything in the household. I didn't need his contribution to survive but the idea of me taking care of him bothered me.

I asked him to put a stop to his wife calling the house. He said he had tried talking to this idiot, but she persisted.

We both arrived home at the same time today. Montel walked to the car and met me.

"That is a nice ride you drive, Nicole."

"Thanks, I like it too."

We walked arm-in-arm to the house. I opened the door, and the phone rang. I went to answer it, and the person on the other end hung up.

"Montel, you've got to do something about Benita calling here and hanging up. I looked at the caller ID and it always lead back to her number. I'm sick of her waking me up in the middle of the night, and even sicker of having to turn my phone off because of her. Anything could happen to my family or friends and they couldn't reach me because my phone is off. The phone rang again. I answered it.

"Nicole, this is Benita."

"And."

"Is my husband there?"

"Look, Benita, I'm real tired of you. Yes, he's here and this is not the lost and found for husbands."

Montel is trying to take the phone from me because I'm irritated and he has no idea what I might say next.

"Benita, you keep calling here for Montel. He has asked you to stop it. I'm asking you to not call here anymore unless there is something wrong with your children."

"I'll call there anytime I damn well please, Miss Thing"

"OK, Why don't I give you the address and we can settle this crap once and for all. You are an ignorant, scandalous woman."

The phone line went dead. Montel had gone in the other room and hung up the phone.

"Nicole, what was that all about?"

"You know what its about."

"You don't do anything about that sow calling here, so I did. If you need to talk to her so badly, go back over there and be with her."

"Calm down baby. You are making too much of this. I love you, not her. I don't want to live there, that's why I left."

I went into the bathroom to wash my face. He came to the door and knocked softly. I heard him, but I wanted to be alone. I didn't answer. I sat down on the toilet with a cold washcloth to my face. I finally felt myself calming down, so I went back out into the living room. I walked over to the bar, where Montel was sitting and poured myself a glass of wine.

"Nicole, I need to talk to you."

"OK, go ahead."

"I need to buy a new car. Mine is always breaking down, and my credit is all jacked up. Would you help me get it? I'd make the payments. I just need you to help me get it."

I knew this was hard for him to ask me, so I told him I needed to think about it. He agreed and said he was going to the lounge to see some friends. He left.

I lay on the sofa and watched TV. I heard him put the key in the door and realized I had fallen asleep.

He sat next to me and said. "Let's go to bed."

I glanced at the clock and saw it was almost 1:00AM.

At work, right before Chantal left, she talked to me about different schools and how to get the most out of the school that I did choose.

Tonight was my holiday party. I had invited a few close friends, no one from the office but Jason and his date whoever that might be. Sheila and her date, my cousin, Avery and her husband, my brother and his wife and a few other people. This would be sort of a going-away party for Sheila. She was leaving for her cruise in a few days.

I finished most of my work and decided to take the rest home to work on.

I needed to stop at the mortgage company to pick up my check from the sale of the house. Gerald was such a jerk about money; I had to have a lawyer put a hold on the distribution of the check. I had the mortgage company write two checks One for me, one for him. He hired an attorney to make sure both checks were equal amounts of money. That was finally over.

Montel had mentioned marriage to me. I'm amazed! He hasn't even talked about his divorce, let alone started any kind of proceedings.

I arrived home and found Montel with a child who was about 7 or 8 years old.

"Hello there." I said.

"Hi." This cute little girl said back.

"I'm Nicole."

"My name is Rajani."

"What a beautiful name." I replied.

Montel kissed me on the lips and gave me a hug.

"I've heard about you and Cherish." I said.

"You have a nice house."

"Thank you. Would you like something to drink?"

"Not now, Nicole, I need to take Rajani home." Montel said. "I wanted Rajani to meet you. Cherish was at her grandmother's, so she didn't get to come."

I said goodbye to Rajani, and she and Montel left.

I started to pick up the few things that were lying around and went into the kitchen to prepare for the party tonight.

"Montel never helped do jack around here." I said to the air, as I picked up a dirty towel in the bathroom. I found a pair of socks on the floor and picked them up, too. I walked to the bedroom and found a pair of slacks on the bed. I picked them up and felt something hard in the pocket.

I looked in the pocket and found a note from some woman that said, I love you Montel but, I know you love Nicole.

How does this person know about me? This wasn't a good sign. Montel obviously told this person about me, or she wouldn't know my name. This woman's name was Alisha. I wouldn't confront Montel just yet. I'm sure he'd only lie anyway. Where was he to get this note? A club, work, where? I hung up the slacks and put the note back in the pocket of the slacks. That dog.

I showered and went into the kitchen to make sure all was ready. I took out this cracked crab and shrimp tray. I put it on the table and got out the china. I hated paper plates and plastic utensils. I put the other appetizers on the table and checked the bar. It was well stocked.

I went into the bedroom and got dressed. I decided to wear a light mint double-breasted button-front jacket with shiffi embroidery and Venice lace at the shoulders and matching slacks. This thing was light colored so I had to be careful about stains. I went back into the living room and turned on the CD player with some jazz to help put me in a festive mood. That note was heavy on my mind.

The doorbell rang and I asked who it was. It was Sheila and her date. His name was Chauncey, and he was all of that. Where did she find these good looking men? They came in. She wore a jumpsuit with pearlized buttons and chain detail and a mock jacket in a seafoam color. The jacket had a shawl collar, and the legs of the pants were wide. She had on these white leather pumps that made her two inches taller. She looked fantastic. Chauncey was dressed nicely as well. I invited them to help themselves to the bar. Sheila made drinks for everybody.

Montel finally got back and had an attitude. I didn't bother to ask what his problem was, because I really didn't give a damn.

The other guests started to arrive, and finally my brother came in with his wife. I hadn't seen him in a few weeks, so we got a chance to talk. He lived over in the East Bay, but worked at night so we didn't get see each other as often as we'd like to.

He met Montel and immediately took a dislike to him.

"Girl, when are you going to get it right? This one, is way out of your league. I hope you know what you're doing."

I ignored him. I was in love and that's all that mattered. He could she be so wrong. He didn't always know what was best for me.

I could tell my guests were having a good time, and so was I. Montel was being the perfect gentleman. He wasn't very social, he stayed off to himself. I went over to him and lead him to the middle of the living room to dance. He put his arms around me and held me tightly. He started to kiss my neck and caress my body in places that were reserved when we were alone. I whispered in his ear to stop it or we would have to excuse ourselves and go to the bedroom to take care of business. Soon the night ended and morning was starting to creep in. I looked at the clock, it was 3:00AM. Everybody decided to leave at once.

Sheila and Chauncey decided to stay. Montel and I went and sat on the sofa. I asked if anyone wanted coffee, but they declined the offer.

We talked and laughed until 4:30AM, and Chauncey decided they should leave and let us go to bed. We said goodnight, and they left. Montel and I went to bed and got to finish our business.

On Sunday, I needed to get up and clean from the party last night. I was lying under Montel's arm, and he reached for me. I got up.

He said to me. "It's like that now?"

I didn't answer. I went into the kitchen and started to clean up. I started thinking about how I was going to invest the money from the sale of the house and it crossed my mind again about how Montel was living off of me. He hadn't even offered to help now that I thought about it.

He came in the kitchen and started to make coffee.

"What's your problem?" he asked.

"My problem is you haven't contributed anything to the running of this household, since you moved in here," I said

"I bought food."

"Yes, once or twice. You tend to eat everyday. There was the rent, PGE, and other things it takes to maintain this household."

"I don't want to hear this crap, Nicole."

I continued to clean. When I finished I went in to get dressed. I couldn't believe he said that to me.

I headed for the door, and Montel said. "I need another car. I know you can get it, so what's the answer?."

I was so stunned by this character's gall. I pushed past him he put his hands around my neck and applied just enough pressure to get my attention. I struggled, but it did no good. He released his grip and I left. I ran to my car and sat there trying to figure out what just happened. I knew, what just happened. That dog just choked me.

I had allowed Montel to use my credit card to get his kids something for Christmas. They thought daddy was the best Santa in the world, but little did they know, Nicole had footed the bills.

I had worked like a mad woman cooking, cleaning, you name it and this scrub came along and didn't do jack. He tried to threaten me into signing for a car.

I went to the lake and walked around it, to clear my head and try to get some perspective on what was going on. I knew Montel was using me, but I wasn't ready to accept that, not just yet.

I headed for home and pulled into the driveway. I didn't see Montel's hunk-a-junk car, so hopefully he'd left. I put the key in the door and went inside. He was gone. I sat at the bar. The door opened and here he came.

"Where did you go?" he asked.

"Out."

"Out where?"

"What is this? You don't own me. I can go where I want to without your permission. You go where ever you want to go."

"I do own you. I own your soul." He laughed.

I have been scared a few times in my life but to be told something like that was beyond my understanding. It's not what he said, but the way he said it. It was like he possessed me. I felt like I was trapped by my own emotions. This was a man who wasn't capable of a healthy relationship with a woman, but a man that wanted to be in total control of my spirit.

"Nicole," he said as he stood in front of me and reached down the front of my shirt. He lifted the shirt, put his mouth on the nipple of my breast and kissed it ever so softly. I felt weak. I knew I shouldn't give in to this pleasure, but maybe he did own my soul.

On our way to the car lot, Montel said. "I'm sorry about this morning. I love you. I would never do anything to hurt you."

Montel found a car that he liked. The salesman made an offer and Montel said the price was wrong and thanked the salesman for his time. We were walking off the lot when the salesman had a better offer. Montel winked at me and we went into the office for me to sign all the paperwork. Montel got all his personal belongings out of the old clunker and we headed home in Montel's new car.

I asked Montel to drop me at the house and he could do whatever he wanted. I went into the house and sat my silly butt down.

How could I be so stupid? I didn't trust Montel, and here I was thousands of dollars more in debt. I dug thorough my purse and found the envelope with the sale of the house check in it. I hadn't even looked to see how much it was for. It was for $500,000.00. I must put this in my safety deposit box until my accountant could give me some investment advice. I planned to buy more property but not with Montel, that's all he needed to see, was me with this much money in my possession.

I went into the kitchen and poured me a shot of bourbon. My hands were shaking. I sat down at the bar and wondered what I had gotten myself into this time.

January 29, my birthday. I got up and found flowers all over the whole house. I didn't remember what time Montel came in last night. I went to bed and fell fast asleep. He must've brought all these flowers in with him. I walked into the kitchen and found him fully showered and dressed. I didn't ask where he went last night.

"Happy birthday, baby," he said.

"Thank you."

"I'd like to take you to dinner tonight to celebrate your birthday."

Just then, the phone rang. I answered and it was Sheila.

"Happy birthday to you, my friend."

"Thank you." I replied.

I'll be over in a while to bring you your present."

"You didn't have to get me anything."

"I know. I saw this and knew you'd love it, so I'll bring it over later and we can drink some champagne. Will you be home?"

"Yes, I'll be here.

"I'll see you later on."

She broke the line. The doorbell rang. Montel answered it. This man was standing at the door and asked for Nicole Adams. I stated I was she. He handed me an envelope. I took it, and he walked away. I had been in the business long enough to know a process server when I saw one.

"These are divorce papers from Gerald." I opened the envelope and saw that I was being sued for divorce. Gerald, the dog he was thought, by having the papers served today, it would ruin my birthday. I jumped, screamed, and cried for joy. I never did do anything with the papers I started.

Montel didn't know what to think. He asked. "What's going on?

I told him about the papers and he smiled.

He said. "You'll finally be mine." He planted kisses all up and down my neck.

Sheila came over, and I told her about the papers.

"That low-lifed sucker. He would try and ruin anything for you. You know Nicole, if it were me, I would've taken that dude to court and squeezed his privates dry."

"No Sheila. I'm just glad to be away from him permanently."

Sheila handed me this big thing. I could tell it was a painting of some kind or another. I unwrapped it and it was the painting I had seen at a Black art fair in the East Bay.

"Thank you." I said as I hugged her.

"Anyway, said Sheila. I leave in two days for the cruise. I'll be gone for 6 weeks."

"Girl, how do you pack for that long? If it was me, I'd have to take 2 steamer trunks."

Sheila laughed. "You should see all the luggage. I went back and bought more pieces to add on to the set I already had. I know I'll be paying extra for the baggage weight. I don't care. Nicole, I just wanted to wish you a happy birthday and tell you goodbye".

We hugged each other, and we both began to cry. "I'll miss you, Sheila."

I'll miss you too Nicole, take care of yourself and I'll call, and give you a number for ship-to-shore calling in case you need me. I'll send a card from every place I can."

"Have a good time."

"I intend to." She left.

Montel was in the bedroom during Sheila's visit. He came out and was very sarcastic.

"What was that all about? I don't know Sheila, but she's a man hater."

"Why is that Montel? Is it because he says what's on her mind and could give less than a thought if you or whoever else likes it or not."

I walked away into my bedroom to dress for this dinner we were supposed to be going to. I decided to wear a black rayon, crepe, cocktail dress. It had a scoop neckline in front, criss-cross stretch bands, and matte gold stars in back. The dress was above the knee, so I decided to wear black leather open-toe pumps. I needed to get in the bathroom and Montel was in there. He took longer than me.

He had purchased a new suit and it looked as though it cost a fortune. Silk shirt, and tie. Whose birthday was it?

He looked at me. "That dress is dangerous girl. Those long legs of yours, and it is fitting those hips like a glove. I might have to kill some mother tonight."

"Montel, you talk real crazy sometimes. Are you that insecure?

"Insecurity has nothing to do with it. That dress is kicking, but it's too short to wear out. You're my woman and I won't have it."

"You stare down other women who dress like this. I don't hear any complaints about their attire."

"There're not my woman."

"What do you mean? This dress is not that short. It's a little above the knee."

"Nicole, you've got long legs. Nice long legs. It shows too much leg. I don't want every man in the place eyeballing your legs. Is that all right with you?"

"No, It's not. What are you really trying to say Montel?"

"I'm saying you're not wearing that short dress out with me."

I looked at this crazy man in total amazement.

"Fine, Montel. I don't have to wear it with you. I can go out by my own self". I got my coat and left.

As I was driving to The Lounge, I felt everything falling apart. I got that sick feeling in my stomach again. I knew something bad was about to happen. Montel needed to get a clue. This was not the year of the fool. His mentality scared me. I'd never known anybody to think the way he thought.

I arrived at the club, and it was packed. I walked over to the bar and found Curtis.

"Nicole, looking good." Where is your escort for the evening?"

"I don't have one. Curtis."

"Nicole, are you still seeing Montel Bradshaw?"

"Yes, Curtis. We live together."

"No bull, Nicole?"

"No bull."

"That dude is possessive. I've seen him with his women over the years. I was surprised to hear you hooked up with that fool."

"Today is my birthday Curtis."

"Happy birthday, Nicole. I hope you have many more. I don't mean to get in your business, but that dude is bad news. His reputation for abusing women is well known." Ask his wife."

Curtis brought over some champagne and wished me a happy birthday again and went back to work. I sat there feeling useless and foolish.

I looked around the club and saw this guy that used to work for the same firm as I did, sitting at a table. I caught his eye and he started to walk over to the bar.

"Hello, Nicole."

"Remember me. My name is Jared Washington."

"Nice to see you Jared. It's been a long time."

"You look fine as can be tonight. Is it a special occasion?"

"Today is my birthday."

"Happy birthday. Is some one joining you this evening?"

"No."

"Well then. Why don't you come over to my table and sit with me. I would love to talk to you."

"Thank you." I said. "I'd like that.

We walked to his table and I sat down. Curtis brought over the bottle of champagne. Jared excused himself to use the bathroom. I watched him walk and he had this proud, gallant, self-confident walk.

I knew this could lead to something, for all my emotions were on the alert. Who needed Montel?

Jared came back to the table and we talked about our admiration of each other's work.

"I heard good things about you from Chantal." Jared said.

"You're like a celebrity yourself. You and Gregory Taylor could start your own fan club."

Jared laughed. His laugh was so sincere, I'd almost forgotten what it was like to have laughter in a conversation. Montel and I never laughed.

"Would you like to dance, Nicole?"

"Yes."

We walked out on the dance floor. Jared was at least 6-4. I was 5-10 with heels on and I had to reach high to put my arms around his neck. I thought about Montel while dancing with Jared. Jared smelled so good.

"Nicole, I like that fragrance you're wearing."

"Thank You."

"I find it hard to believe you're here all alone on your birthday."

"I had other plans but they got jacked up, so here I am"

I could feel Jared's hands on the lower part of my back while we danced to this slow song. He was holding me tighter and tighter as the song played and I was starting to really get into this dance. Finally the song was over, but he didn't move his hands. He kissed me on the lips and thanked me for the dance. We went back to the table.

We talked some more about our future plans. I told him I planned to attend law school as soon as possible. He gave me his card and told me to give him a call when I had finalized everything. He stated he could be of great assistance in helping me.

I thanked him for helping make my birthday one to be remembered and explained I had to get home. He walked me to my car and I knew there was some kind of chemistry that passed between us. I let him kiss me goodnight. The power of that kiss went through my entire nervous system. My emotional state of being went on overload.

I saw Montel's car, as I pulled up in the driveway. I saw the house was dark from the street, so I assumed Montel was asleep, and because he was angry with me, he turned off all the lights.

I walked to the door, and the door was open. He grabbed me by the hair and pulled me inside the door. He flipped on a light and started to slug me with his fist in the face, while calling me all kinds of names.

"Where were you tramp? Who do you think you are to walk out on me?"

I had flashbacks to when Gerald and I were going through this very thing. I broke away from Montel and picked up the telephone to call 911. He planned for that. I couldn't get a dial tone. He mentioned he took the extension off the hook just in case I made that move.

Montel, after hitting me a couple more times, pulled off my dress and ripped it into pieces.

"Tramp, you won't wear this again."

I ran to my room and grabbed a bathrobe. He followed me and pushed me down on the floor.

"Come here, tramp. I'll give you just what you want."

This was the ultimate humiliation. Montel didn't drink much, but his manner was so bizarre. After struggling with him, he saw he couldn't get an erection, so he went in the living room.

I went into the bathroom and looked in the mirror. Beyond the tears was the beginning of a black eye and a swollen face. I went to the refrigerator and took some ice out of the freezer and put some in a towel and held it to my face.

Montel was sitting on the sofa with a mirror and a hundred-dollar bill snorting cocaine.

"This is the best girl in town". "This girl won't do you wrong". He said in a cocaine stupor.

I looked at this freak in horror. This was a crazed cokehead I had living in my house.

I got up the next morning, running late for work. My face was slightly swollen and luckily I didn't have a black eye. I saw Montel had slept on the sofa. I'm going to put his butt out of my house today. That sorry excuse of a human being lives here debt free but has money to buy drugs.

I was just about ready to leave for work when the phone rang. It was Benita, Montel's wife.

"Yes."

"Look Nicole, I know you don't think much of me, and I'm sorry for playing the stupid phone games with you, but I would like to talk to you."

"Talk to me about what?"

"You and Montel."

"What does that have to do with you?"

"Nothing. My reason is because you seemed to be a nice person, so my kids said, and I'm aware, you spent your money so they could have a nice Christmas."

"OK," I said.

"Can we meet sometime?" she asked. "What I have to say is of importance to you. I don't want Montel back, because he's no good. He has caused me nothing but grief since the day I got involved with him."

"Benita, I'm not comfortable talking to you, but since you made the effort I'll meet with you. There's one thing I'd like to know about Montel."

"What is it?" she asked.

"Is Montel a coke-head?"

"No, it's not a daily thing with him. But he does enjoy doing it. It has been over the years when he loves a woman and can't totally dominate her; he'll use drugs to justify his insecurity. You're an independent woman and he likes that more than anything, that way he can take his money and spend it anyway he wants, as long as he knows you'll take care of business for him."

"Benita, one other thing. Did Montel beat on you during your marriage?"

"Yes". I put him out. When he told me he was moving with you, I had all the locks changed, packed up all his stuff and took it to his mama's house. I never want his sorry butt to come back into my life."

"Benita, I can meet with you today. Here is my work number, call me and confirm a time."

"OK, Nicole I will", she said. The connection was broken.

I headed for the job and couldn't concentrate on driving for thinking about last night's events. What could Benita possibly tell me that I didn't already know? After last night, nothing would surprise me about that loser.

As I was driving along, I saw Montel driving towards me with some woman in the car with him. He honked and waved. I continued on my way to work. That dog was getting out of my house and out of that car today. *The nerve of this trick.* My head was spinning.

I turned around and headed back to the house. I called Jason from the cell phone to let him know I wouldn't be in today. I could be reached at home and have all my messages sent to my voice mail.

I called Benita back and she said she could meet me in an hour. We agreed to meet at a coffee shop on the El Camino.

I drove to the restaurant, and I forgot to ask what she would have on. I had never seen her in person, and she had never seen me. We found each other with no problem, since we were the only ones in the place at the time. I offered to buy coffee, and she accepted.

"Nicole, my purpose in telling you this is to spare you heartache."

"Don't beat around the bush. Benita, just tell me."

"OK, here goes. I don't know if Montel mentioned to you that I was pregnant when we got married."

"Yes, he told me about that."

Well, anyway, the woman he was dating and engaged to marry before me is here in California staying at his mama's house."

"OK, so what."

"He has been seeing her behind your back."

"I just saw Montel with a woman in the car with him."

"I have a good relationship with his parents because of the children. She made arrangements to come here, and he helped plan it. He let's her use his new car. I know the car has to be registered to you. Nobody in their right mind would give that loser credit, cause he doesn't pay his bills."

"Yes, I signed for the car, like a fool."

"I'm telling you this, because he thinks he's so slick with his act, not to hurt you. I'll be filing for divorce soon, and whoever wants him, God bless and keep them."

I finished my coffee while listening to Benita tell me things that I expected to hear. How Montel didn't pay his bills, beat his wife, a womanizer, she had an endless list. I finally stopped her. I had heard enough.

I remembered what Sheila said about Montel, and what my brother said. How could I keep making these same stupid choices in men? Was my emotional makeup so jacked until I'd lost the ability to make sound, and reasonable judgment in a mate?

I could see the pain in Benita's eyes. I believed she told me these things for the reasons she stated. She said she had to leave and I just sat there staring into space trying to absorb the conversation we had.

I saw things in a different light now. I would confront Montel later. I decided to go to work. Right now, I needed my job to help me make sense of my life.

I arrived at work and informed Jason to screen my calls. He said he understood. I got busy on my research, and the remainder of the day flew by. Jason stuck his head in the door and informed me he was leaving for the day. I looked at the clock and saw it was almost 6:00PM. I told him goodnight, and he left. I cleared things at my desk and headed for home and the showdown.

As I pulled into the driveway, I saw Montel's car was there. I couldn't deal with him. I went into the house. My anger had the best of me, but I walked straight to my bedroom. He was in the kitchen.

"Are you going to make dinner"?

I laughed out loud.

"Better get that woman, you were riding around this morning, to cook you some dinner."

"There you go, Nicole, you don't even know who that was."

"No, I don't, and furthermore, I don't give a damn. I want you out of here. You're no good. I don't want you in my house. It was a mistake to allow you to stay here."

"Look Nicole, I know I shouldn't have hit you, but you have this arrogant attitude. I was so mad that you walked out on me."

"And that's how you deal with it? Look, I want you out of here. I don't care what your reasons are. Pack up your stuff and go. I made a mistake with that car as well. You used force to try and intimidate me to do things for you. I don't like that. What kind of a man are you?"

He looked at me and spit in my face. I walked away from him and went into the bedroom to wash my face. I was beside myself. I had never had anyone to spit in my face before. I picked up my keys and purse and went out to my car to use the cell phone to call 911. I explained to them what I wanted done. The police said they would be there momentarily. I waited at my car for them to accompany me back inside my house. They arrived in 2 minutes.

I knew the police team that arrived.

"Nicole, what's going on?" Said Officer Bennett.

"Hello, Stan." I explained to him, and they followed me back in the house.

Montel was still there. Montel looked like he could kill me. The police officer asked Montel if he had any papers showing his rights of occupancy. He did not. They told him he had to leave. He started to gather his things. They asked if I wanted them to stay until he was gone, and I said Yes, also I wanted my keys back.

While they were watching him, I went into the back room with the telephone and called a locksmith. I wasn't taking any chances with this crazy man.

Officer Bennett asked if there had been any domestic violence. I lied and said no. I just wanted Montel out of there. He had hurt me, but I still loved him. *Jesus, when was I going to get it?*

How could you tell me you love me one night and humiliate me by spitting in my face? I wouldn't spit in a dog's face.

Finally, Montel had his things and was walking out the door.

"Before you go, I have something to say to you. That car is in my name, you miss one payment, and I'll find it and take it away from you."

"Screw you." he said.

I went to bed and cried myself to sleep.

I got up and remembered what happened a few hours ago. I sat at the bar and poured myself a soda. I found my phone book and punched the number for Morrison Davis. He was a private investigator, I knew from the firm. He was not there, so I left a message on his voice mail.

Montel, the dog, he was. I was going to get Morrison to do a background check on Montel for me. I should've had it done the first time I laid eyes on that loser. I was going to have that car picked up and sold. How could I be so stupid as to sign anything for that loser?

I took a shower. After the shower, I lay across the bed and could smell Montel's scent. I stripped everything off the bed, turned over the mattress, and put brand new linen on the bed. That felt better. No Montel odor, just the smell of new linen. I slept like a baby.

I got up the next morning and dressed for work. I walked outside and found my car window was broken. I hadn't set the car alarm. I knew Montel had done this. I couldn't prove it, so I brushed the broken glass off the seat and drove on to work.

I got to the office and went straight to my office. I called my insurance company, and they would send someone over right away to pick up the car to have the window fixed. They stated they could have it done in a few hours.

Next thing I did was start typing up the papers for a temporary restraining order. I got done with that and had Jason take them over to the courthouse to have them filed. I would have the process server, serve Montel at his place of employment.

He took the papers, and I could see this look of concern on his face but he didn't say anything. That's what I liked about him. He didn't interfere in my personal business.

I checked my voice mail and found a message from Morrison. I punched his number. This time he answered.

"Nicole Adams. How have you been?"

"I've been fine. Listen, I need you to do a background check on a Montel Bradshaw. I don't have an address."

"That's OK. Do you have a social security number?"

"Yes. I did have it."

I copied it off of a paycheck stub Montel had laid on the dresser. I did that after signing for that car. I didn't know if I'd ever need it or not but just in case. I may not have lost all my mind.

"By the way Nicole, I hear Chantal left."

"Yes, she did."

"Have you heard from her?"

"No, not at all. Morrison, this is a personal case, I'm asking you to work on for me, so just send me the bill when you're done."

He laughed. "Nicole, this one is on the house. I appreciate the work you did for me sometime back. Consider us even."

"You've got a deal."

I said. "I'll be in touch in a week or so."

"Exactly what do you want to find out about Montel Bradshaw?"

"Everything you can."

He didn't mince words. He just said "Done." and hung up the phone.

Most everything at work was completed, so I decided to take a break. The phone buzzed and Jason informed me they delivered my car. That made me happy. I bet I'd turn the alarm on from now on. I decided to head for home and sort out where to go from here.

As I walked out to my car I spotted Jared Washington. He came over, and we talked about the night at the lounge. I didn't remember him being as tall. He was very handsome. He was dressed to kill. I could tell by his whole demeanor that he was a class act. This was a gentleman.

I inquired about his family. He told me he was divorced and had two children that lived out of state. His children came out generally during the school breaks and the summertime.

He invited me to have a drink or coffee, but I declined the offer. I would have loved to have a drink with Jared but I didn't trust myself in making choices about men. That last choice I made was too destructive. Obviously I wasn't ready to make any decisions regarding men.

He smiled, and I could tell one day I might take him up on his offer. I felt better. The pain of what Montel did to me wasn't as overpowering as I thought.

He touched my hand, and said. "You have a pleasant evening, and I hope to see you again soon."

I arrived home and found a message on the machine from Morrison. I called him back, and he suggested I come over to his office. I asked if he could send a messenger with the report. He said sure. The papers would be there in an hour.

I got undressed, and the buzzer rang. I asked who it was, and it was Montel. I don't dare let this psycho in.

He said. "Nicole, I need to talk to you."

"Use the phone you low-life."

"Open the door, Nicole or I will stay here all night."

"Suit your crazy self Montel. I had a restraining order issued on you today. Did you get your copy?"

"Yeah, you b———. I got it."

"So stay there while I call the police."

I didn't hear anything more, so I waited for a few minutes longer. I looked out the window and saw him driving away.

I put on a bathrobe and poured a glass of wine. I sat down on the sofa to wait for the messenger to come. I thought, let Montel keep that car until he misses one payment. That's a stupid idea. That car is in your name. You're the one responsible if anything happens.

I picked up the phone and asked for Morrison's office again. He answered.

"This is Nicole again."

"Hey what's up?"

"I need to hire you this time."

"What can I do for you?"

"I need you to pick up a car for me."

"You mean like, repossess it?"

"You got it."

"Here are the addresses where the car might be located and the times it might be there."

I gave him description, color, and make, license plate number. He said he'd put somebody on it right away and I could expect results in 72 hours. I told him to bill me.

The buzzer rang again. I asked who it was, and he said a messenger from the detective agency. I opened the door to let him in. I walked to the door and looked out the peephole to make sure. I saw this young Black dude with a manila envelope, so I opened the door. He handed it to me and I handed him 10 dollars.

He said. "Thank you lady." and walked away.

I took the envelope, and made another drink, and had a seat at the bar. The envelope was not very full, so maybe that was a good sign. I held the envelope for a minute and thought that whatever the contents, it would change my relationship with Montel forever. Our relationship, or whatever that was, all ties had already been severed. I thought about how I felt about him, the way he made me feel. I could feel his touch. I could still smell him on me. It would be a while before I was emotionally rid of Montel.

I had been through too many changes already with men. No wonder Sheila and so many other women I talked to had such cynical attitudes towards men. Montel had the best I could give to anyone. All my love.

I opened the envelope and started to read the report. The report said Montel had been arrested 7 times for domestic abuse. He had been arrested for not paying income tax. He had been arrested for trying to cash a stolen check. He had been evicted from 4 apartment complexes. He was arrested for possession of a controlled substance. Those charges were dropped. A complaint had been filed for Senior abuse on an elderly parent. I read this, and my stomach felt sick. Morrison even did a credit check on Montel. The credit report was one of the worst I'd ever seen. He made bills and never bothered to pay them. I would imagine, he had used many women for credit and ruined their credit history, like he would do mine if I didn't do something about it.

The phone rang. I answered it and it was Morrison.

"Nicole, when I find this car, where do you want me to take it?"

"Bring it to my address." I told him. "I can handle it from there."

"Thanks," he said and hung up.

I called my cousin and asked if I could use her garage for a few days. She agreed.

I sipped my drink and absorbed all I read. JESUS is all I could say. Love sure wasn't easy. I finished my drink and decided to go to bed. I could feel Montel's arms around me. I could sense his presence in the room. I decided that it was OK to hurt and mourn this loss. It was his loss. I tried to make it something beautiful and special, and he took advantage. I fell asleep.

I woke up and found that I wasn't depressed. I didn't feel like a victim this time around. I picked up the newspaper and found the number to the Cars for Sale section. I punched in the number and informed the person that I had a car to sell. They stated I needed a bankcard to place the ad. I gave them my credit card number. The ad would run for 7 days. I hung-up the phone and got dressed for work.

I arrived at work, and there was a message from Morrison. I phoned him back, and he said he had the car at his office. I could pick it up at anytime. I told him I would be over within the hour. I found a message from Montel. I threw it away before reading it. I wasn't returning any of his phone calls. I knew exactly what he wanted to say.

I called my cousin to let her know I would be over in a while.

I had a meeting that afternoon about a case. I tried to prepare all the outlines, but I couldn't concentrate. Jason buzzed me and said that

Jared Washington was on the line. He invited me to lunch. I accepted. I told him I could meet after 2:00PM

He said, "I'll pick you up at your office."

"OK, see you then."

I called my brother to drive my car for me. He agreed to do that. I explained what happened. I waited for "I told you so," but he never said a word.

"I'm just glad you cancelled that dude. He was a loser."

We arrived at my cousins and left the car. I dropped my brother off at home and headed back to the office for lunch with Jared. I was getting excited.

I got back to work, and there sat Montel.

"Nicole, I need to talk to you."

I stood a distance from him.

"Somebody stole the car from the parking lot last night while I was at work."

Here stood this butthead with this smug look on his face.

"What do you propose me to do about it Montel? Did you report it to the police?"

"No, I didn't yet."

"Why is that Montel?"

"I called you last night, and this morning, but you refused to return my calls. Nicole, since you're so upstanding, I figured you could handle it. It's in your name, Miss high and mighty. You're responsible for it.

"Excuse me," said Jared.

Where did he come from? I wondered, who cared. He was my Black knight, and he looked like he was ready to do battle with this fool.

"I don't know what this is all about, but I know disrespecting this lady will not be tolerated."

"Who are you?" asked Montel.

"I'm a colleague of Nicole's said Jared, as he opened his coat just enough to flash a shoulder holster that contained a 9mm.

Montel looked at me then at Jared.

"You sure didn't let your bed get cold did you, Nicole?"

Before I could say anything, Jared asked Montel to leave.

"Look man. I would advise you to leave. You are on private property and could be arrested for trespassing and a variety of other charges. I also understand there is a restraining order in effect against you."

Montel talked crap, but Jared stood his ground. Montel finally started to walk away, and I could tell he was a coward when it came to dealing with another man.

I hugged Jared and thanked him for coming to my aid.

I headed back to the office, accompanied by Jared, and we went to lunch. I told Jared all that happened between Montel and me. He just listened. He didn't pass judgment or give his personal views.

"Jared, I asked. "Do you always carry a gun?"

" Oh Yes. I never leave home without it. The American Express card don't mean jack. I'm an officer of the court and I've made lots of enemies over the years because of what I do. I feel a little more secure, when I'm armed."

"The only thing I have to say about your ex-friend is that he's a user. I have a mother, sisters, and daughters. I wouldn't want them to get involved with anyone like him."

"How did you know about the restraining order?"

"I was at the courthouse the day the papers were filed, so I saw them and I have friends that work in that office. You're a celebrity around town and when they saw your name it peeked their interest even more. Don't you know you inspire women to be strong and not take that crap from anyone?"

I never thought about that. I was only trying to survive not inspire anybody.

"Nicole, you're a nice lady, and I see good things in the future for you."

"Is that right?"

"Yes in deed," he said with a smile and a wink of those gorgeous eyes.

We finished lunch. We sat there over coffee and laughed and talked and had a good time. I felt something was happening between us but I didn't dare pursue it. This time I would go nice and slow. If he wanted me, he'd be around.

I arrived back at work, and there was a message for the sale of the car. I called the person back and made arrangements to meet. They decided to purchase the car. I sold it at a loss, but anything was better than letting it get repossessed. I could move on.

I decided to call Jared's office, and his secretary said his schedule was open later today. I arrived at his office, and we talked about what he did and what I would do if I worked with him. I told him I'd think about it. We made plans to have dinner later in the evening.

On the way home, I made a mental list of all the things I needed to do. I had sent off for my former college transcripts and was waiting for them to arrive. Jared offered to make some phone calls to various schools he knew. I appreciated that.

I got home and found the transcripts waiting for me in the mailbox. I kicked my shoes off and started to fill out an application I obtained for U.C. Berkeley. I also had an application for Stanford. Jared was going to email me over 4 more applications within a couple of hours. He was amazing.

All of a sudden I heard my car alarm go off. I ran to my bedroom and got the cordless phone in case I needed it. I hit 911 in the memory

I looked out the window and there was Montel with a gun, waving it in the air. I hit the speed dial. The police were there in 1 minute. After I saw them talking to Montel. I went to the bedroom and got a copy of the restraining order. I showed it to the police and they handcuffed him and put him in the police car.

"You screwed up my life Nicole. You will pay." Montel said.

Both policemen looked at me, then looked at Montel.

"Bradshaw" said one of the policemen, "You screwed yourself by violating this order of protection. You shouldn't be on this property or near this woman. You're looking for trouble, carrying a loaded gun. You screwed yourself".

The messenger arrived with the applications and I was so excited. I'm really going to do this I thought to myself.

Jared would be here soon to pick me up for dinner.

I showered and got dressed. Jared was on time. I invited him in and we decided to have a drink before dinner.

There were many things I found attractive about Jared. He was attentive, had a sense of humor, he cared about what I felt. The list went on and on. He wasn't too good to be true, he was real. I found myself liking him more than I wanted to. This time it was a healthy situation. I knew it was too soon to get involved with anyone and I had a lot of work to do within myself. I had issues and I needed time to figure out what they were and find resolution.

We talked so long it was too late for dinner. I ended up making eggs and bacon. Jared acted like it was a gourmet meal. I liked that, it made me feel good. He was a gentleman. He made no moves to try and spend the night or even go in my bedroom. He said he had an early meeting and needed to get home and get some rest. He kissed me on the cheek goodnight and left.

I got in bed and memories of Montel came flooding back. It's going to be a while before I forgot the passion filled nights we had. If that kind of passion was unhealthy, bring me some more of it. Not.

The last day of the week had finally arrived. I decided I'd work 1/2 a day and go home and complete my applications so they could be mailed.

I began to fill out the applications and started to sing to myself. I thanked God and all the people who encouraged me to go as far as my motivation would take me. I knew that troubles don't last always and joy does come in the morning.

My divorce from Gerald was final, and I hadn't heard from Montel since that day the police took him away. I heard he moved in with somebody else in San Francisco.

Sheila was due back any day; I couldn't wait to tell her all that had happened since she left.

I finally completed the applications and decided to walk to the post office to mail them. As I was walking through the Rose Garden, I noticed all the rose bushes had been pruned. Not a bud to be seen.

I saw an elderly lady that was distressed and in tears.

I asked, "What's wrong"?

She stated her husband loved this Rose Garden. He recently passed away and she didn't find life worth living anymore. As she told me her story, I listened. What a good man her husband must have been. She softly said, her husband always told her to take time to smell the roses.

She looked at me and said, "How can you smell the roses if the tops have been cut off?"

About the Author

She was inspired to write based on personal life experiences as well as situations of sister friends. Writing this story has been an emotional cleansing, an unpacking of excessive baggage and a creative writing buffet of emotion.

She has been published on the Internet in 1999 as an electronic book. The site was setup for the reader to give feedback and make comments on the book. This proved to be a valuable format. Comments came from all across the country. Men and women could relate to the story line. A number of requests were made to have the paper version of the book.

www.ingramcontent.com/pod-product-compliance
Lightning Source LLC
Chambersburg PA
CBHW030347290526
45785CB00004B/1635